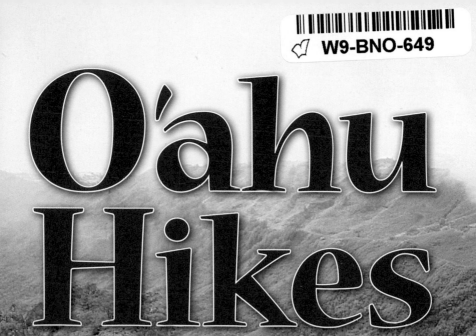

O'ahu Hikes

The Best Hikes and Walks on the Island

Yvonne Harris

LONE
PINE

The Publisher: Lone Pine Publishing
10145 – 81 Avenue
Edmonton, AB T6E 1W9
Website: www.lonepinepublishing.com

Library and Archives Canada Cataloguing in Publication

Harris, Yvonne, 1935–
Oahu hikes / Yvonne Harris.

Includes index.
ISBN-13: 978-1-55105-355-4
ISBN-10: 1-55105-355-1

    1. Hiking—Hawaii—Oahu—Guidebooks. 2. Trails—Hawaii—Oahu—Guidebooks.
3. Oahu (Hawaii)—Guidebooks. I. Title.
GV199.42.H32O147 2007   919.6904'42   C2007-903349-0

Editorial Director: Nancy Foulds
Project Editor: Volker Bodegom, Gary Whyte, Nicholle Carrière
Photo Coordinator: Carol Woo
Production Manager: Gene Longson
Book Design: Heather Markham
Book Layout: Heather Markham, Volker Bodegom
Production Support and Charts: Michael Cooke, Trina Koscielnuk
Cover Design: Gerry Dotto
Cartography: Volker Bodegom

Photos are by Yvonne and Paul Harris, except the following: Byron Kirkham (pp. 14, 32, 43, 80, 144, 228a).

We acknowledge the financial support of the Government of Canada through the Book Publishing Industry Development Program (BPIDP) for our publishing activities.

PC: 16

DISCLAIMER

Although the hikes in this guide are relatively easy, hiking entails an element of risk. Weather, erosion and other conditions may change routes, so use this book as a guide only and make your own judgment about the risks. It is your responsibility to make yourself aware of changes (such as new accesses or closed trails) or hazards that might have occurred since this guide was researched and to be aware of daily changes in weather that may affect your safety on the hikes.

This book serves as a guide only, and it remains the sole responsibility of readers to determine which hikes are appropriate for their skill and fitness levels and those of their hiking group. The author and publisher cannot be held responsible for any thefts, problems, injuries or misfortunes that occur from use of the material in this book.

ACKNOWLEDGMENTS

To my husband, Paul, who was my companion on these hikes, and to the staff at Lone Pine Publishing for editing, layout and guidance.

To the generous Hawai'ian people who assisted us throughout our research. We especially thank Bianca Yamamoto for driving us back to our vehicle when we came off the 10-mile hike on the Maunawili Demonstration Trail.

To the staff members at the Division of State Parks who provided assistance and information. I especially wish to thank Parks official, Aaron Lowe, who responded to my questions and provided excellent advice.

TABLE OF CONTENTS

THE HIKES

PREFACE

While this book was being written, my husband and I lived in the subarctic climate of Whitehorse, Yukon, where the lake ice does not break up until June. The winters in Canada's North are cold and dark, and the temperature in one small Yukon community was measured at –88°F, the lowest ever recorded in the world!

We recently spent two years living on the Arctic Circle in Pangnirtung, a small aboriginal village in Canada's Eastern Arctic. In this remote village, my husband and I regularly hiked up the steep mountains that surround Pangnirtung Fiord. We spent several days hiking in Auyuittuq National Park, one of the most spectacular hiking areas in the world.

When Lone Pine Publishing asked me to write a hiking guide for O'ahu, my hiking boots, GPS receiver and sunscreen were packed before the publishers could give it another thought. You see, among the many other sports I like to do, I love to hike. I am not one of those strapping young people capable of bounding up steep ridges, sleeping in the torrential rain and hiking 30 miles in a day. But, like many of the tourists to O'ahu, I am a healthy and active senior.

To research this guide, my husband and I hiked each trail, sometimes redoing a specific hike several times to ensure accuracy. After hiking in the cold, treeless tundra of the Arctic, the tropical forests of Hawai'i were a wonderful change.

My attraction to Hawai'i began with my first visit in 1999. We flew from Whitehorse, Yukon, which was in the clutches of the arctic winter, and arrived on O'ahu at midnight. The temperature change from our home in the North to O'ahu was 80°F.

We drove over the Ko'olau Range to our rented beach house on the windward side of the island. Gentle waves rolled ashore, and, under the moonlight and stars, I could make out the long stretch of Lanikai's white sand beach. I waded into the warm ocean water and understood why Hawai'i is called paradise.

Yvonne Harris on the Hawai'ian Islands

Author and husband, Paul, on a hike to the Arctic Circle, Baffin Island.

INTRODUCTION

The trails and strolls in this book are reasonably easy, and none require overnight camping. Most of them are suitable for families with young children, and all of them are suitable for fit seniors. There are short, easy strolls, remote hikes along the spectacular ocean side of Oʻahu's North Shore, trips along the mountain ridges with breathtaking views of both sides of the island, and peaceful, almost spiritual strolls to the sacred and ancient shrines of the indigenous Hawaiʻians.

This guide is intended for the beginner and intermediate hiker. For experienced back-country hikers and mountaineers, I recommend Stuart Ball's *Hiking Guide to Oʻahu*.

Travelers are searching for more diverse activities during their vacations. Visitors in the 1950s and 1960s chose Waikīkī beach, restaurants and nightlife, but today's tourists are increasingly becoming interested in backcountry hiking as a way to find peace and quiet and to learn about the flora and fauna in the remote regions of Oʻahu. Hawaiʻi's state planners have been trying to direct tourism away from overused sites to other activities— hiking, birdwatching, photography and visits to remote extinct volcanoes and hidden waterfalls. It is my hope that this hiking guide will help support some of the demand for this expanding ecotourism.

How To Use This Guide

Hiking Regions

In this guide, the hikes and strolls are arranged by area: Honolulu Region, East Oʻahu, North Shore, West-Central Oʻahu and Urban Strolls. Check p. 236 for an alphabetical listing.

Honolulu Region

Located in the southwest of Oʻahu, Honolulu is the island's most popular tourist destination. The climate here is dry and sunny. Honolulu is an ideal central location for getting to the famous hike up the walls of Diamond Head crater and for hiking the extensive network of trails on the slopes leading to the Koʻolau Range. It is only a short 2-mile drive to the popular Mānoa Falls Trail and to a network of trails in the Makiki system. Honolulu, known worldwide for the surfing, swimming, canoeing and sunbathing at Waikīkī Beach, is also ideal for the leisurely urban and beach strolls described in this guide.

East Oʻahu

Visit the windward side of the island and enjoy the charming communities of Lanikai, Kailua and Kāneʻohe, which offer a range of services and easy access to the beaches for kayaking, swimming and windsurfing. The hiking trails are an hour or two drive from Waikīkī. The windward side receives more rainfall than the Honolulu area, and several hiking trails feature deep ravines with beautiful streams and waterfalls. East Oʻahu is also the location of the Polynesian Culture Center, where visitors can learn about the first inhabitants of this beautiful island.

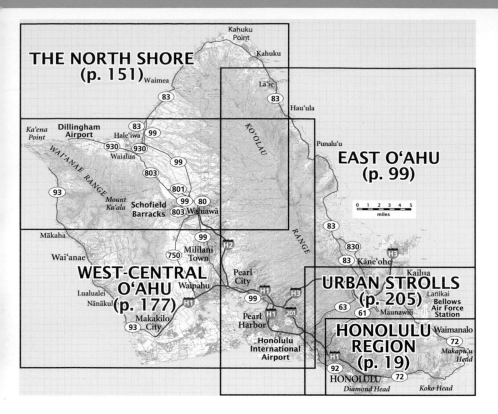

North Shore

The 44-mile drive from Honolulu to the North Shore is well worth the effort, because this region offers the most spectacular hike featured in this guide. You can include a visit to the famous ‘Ehukai surfing beach and its Banzai Pipeline, see young Hawai‘ians dive into a tropical pool located at the Waimea Valley and Adventure Park, walk around the Pu‘u o Mahuka Heiau (a sacred ancient temple above Waimea Bay) and visit the funky town of Hale‘iwa.

West-Central O‘ahu

The west-central hikes include the breathtaking walk to Ka‘ena Point, the high ridge loop in the Wai‘anae Range and a peaceful valley walk in the ‘Aiea region.

Urban Strolls

Five more leisurely strolls are also described in this guide: two in Waikīkī, one each along the beaches of Kailua and Lanikai and one through a peaceful botanical garden in Kāne‘ohe.

Maps

The maps in this guide provide a general guideline for the location of a trail and should not be used for detailed navigation. For greater detail, order the 1:24,000 scale USGS topographical maps.

USGS Information Services
Box 25286
Denver, CO 80225
1-800-HELP-MAP
http://ask.usgs.gov/prices/ordering_info.
html

Pacific Map Center
560 North Nimitz Highway, Suite 206a
Honolulu, HI 96817
Phone: (808) 545-3600; Fax: (808) 545-
1700
http://www.pacmapctr@worldnet.att.net
Email: pacmapctr@worldnet.att.net

Below are the Hawai'ian government
offices that provide trail maps, permits
and updates on trail conditions. Prior to
your hike, check with the Hawai'ian
officials to determine if the trail is still
open. Access to a trail may be terminated
by the landowner, closed by officials or
rerouted because of natural forces. For
maps of trails, permits and the most
recent information contact:

**Department of Land and Natural
Resources**
Division of Forestry and Wildlife
1151 Punchbowl Street, Room 325
Honolulu, HI 96813
http://www.hawaii.gov/dlnr/Welcome.
html
Email: dlnr@hawaii.gov

For car camping or use of cabins, maps
and trail information for state park trails,
contact:

**Department of Land and Natural
Resources**
Division of State Parks, O'ahu District
1151 Punchbowl Street, Room 310
Honolulu, HI 96813

Camping information: (808) 587-0300
Hiking information: (808) 587-0166

Na Ala Hele (NAH) is the Hawai'i
Statewide Trails and Access Program
created in response to concerns about
maintaining access to trails.

http://www.hawaiitrails.org/
Phone: (808) 973-9782
Email: alowe@hawaii.rr.com

Information on O'ahu hiking may also
be available from the following local
organizations:

Hawai'ian Trail and Mountain Club
Phone: (808) 674-1459
http://htmclub.org/index.html

Hawai'i Nature Center
http://www.hawaiinaturecenter.org/
Phone: (808) 955-0100 or toll free
(888) 955-0104

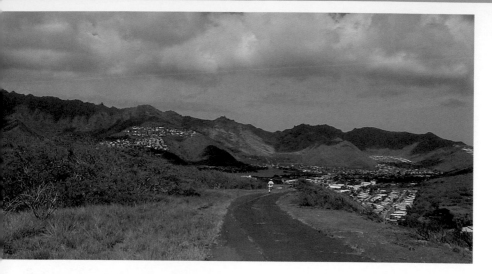

Vehicle Access to the Trailhead

Because there is limited signage for many of the trails and because the roads leading up the mountain slopes are circuitous, one of the most difficult challenges is finding the trailhead. This guide provides route direction and the approximate distance from Waikīkī to the trailhead. Pick up a good map book such as the *Rand McNally Street Guide: Oʻahu*. If you have access to the Internet, you can check routes on a site such as http://www.mapquest.com.

As you drive around Oʻahu, you will find that a highway may change names while keeping the same number or vice versa, and the signage is currently being updated, so we have sought to provide both name and number in the access descriptions. We are using the abbreviation SR (State Route) with state highway numbers, but some other sources use HI instead, and highway signs normally give just the number.

When parking in residential areas, please be respectful of the inhabitants and watch for no-parking zones. Note that it is illegal to park within 4 feet of a driveway or alongside a red-marked curb.

Bus Access to the Trailhead

If time permits, taking TheBus is a preferable alternative to a private vehicle. You won't have to contend with finding your way through the winding, often poorly marked streets and roads of Oʻahu, and you needn't worry about break-ins or vandalism. TheBus provides service to all communities on Oʻahu and circles the entire island with the exception of the most westerly point. For a free bus schedule, visit the office at the following address, check the website or send a stamped, self-addressed envelope (U.S. postage or enclose international reply coupons).

ThcBus, Oʻahu Transit Services, Inc.
811 Middle Street
Honolulu, HI 96819
Phone: (808) 848-5555
http://www.thebus.org/

A Portrait of O'ahu

Seventy million years ago, a rupture in the Pacific Plate allowed molten lava to spurt through weak areas on the ocean floor, 15,000 feet below the ocean's surface. The underwater volcanoes here piled lava onto lava until the formation was high enough to break through the ocean's surface. O'ahu, the second of the Hawai'ian Islands to form, was born out of two mountain ranges—the Wai'anae Range to the northwest and the Ko'olau Range to the southeast. The Hawai'ian Archipelago is the longest island chain in the world, stretching 1600 miles from the Kure Atoll to the Hawai'ian Islands.

O'ahu extends over nearly 600 square miles. Three-quarters of the state's population resides on O'ahu, and the island is the destination of choice for most of the six million tourists who visit Hawai'i each year.

Climate

The average summer temperature in Honolulu is 80–85°F, with winter lows of 70–75°F. The windward, or eastern, part of O'ahu is slightly more moderate, with summer highs of 80–82°F and winter lows of 62–70°F.

Winter is slightly wetter than summer. Trade winds from the east moderate the climate. At times, O'ahu is hit by the *kona* winds from the south, bringing hot, humid weather. Winter storms, also from the south, can be strong enough to cause damage.

Remember that you are close to the equator, where darkness falls quickly, at about the same time year-round. Plan to finish the day's hiking well before the 6:00 PM nightfall.

Plants and Animals

Few of the world's terrestrial sites are more isolated than Hawai'i—the islands are some 1850 miles from the nearest other islands (the Marquesas in French Polynesia). Except for animal species brought to O'ahu (pigs, mongooses and rats), there are no wild mammals. There are no freshwater fish, and there are no snakes.

Wild plants and animals fall into four groups:

- *Endemic:* species found only in Hawai'i and nowhere else. For example, of the 1894 species of flowering plants in Hawai'i, 45 percent (850) are endemic.

- *Indigenous:* species that colonized the islands before the arrival of humans and still grow elsewhere.

• *Polynesian:* species introduced by the ancient Polynesian settlers.

• *Alien (also called introduced, exotic or invasive):* species that became naturalized following European contact in 1778.

Hawai'ian birds are being threatened by mongooses, feral cats and rats brought to the islands. Similarly, endemic, indigenous and Polynesian plants are being threatened by the spread of alien plant species that outcompete them.

Most of the trail descriptions in this guide include a list of plants to look for. Each plant is described once in the guide, and the page number of the description is listed in the index of plants on p. 237.

Hawai'ian Sovereignty and Culture

The Hawai'ians were a self-sufficient society with well-organized land and political systems before the arrival of the first Europeans, under British explorer Captain James Cook, in 1778. Between 1826 and 1893, the United States government recognized the Hawai'ian government, which was led by a long-established line of royalty. The situation changed in 1893, when reigning Queen Lili'oukalani was dethroned and the government of Hawai'i was taken over by the United States. In 1959, Hawai'i became a state. Even today, there remains a strong sovereignty movement throughout Hawai'i.

A Few Key Facts

The population of the State of Hawai'i was 1.3 million in 2005; 6.6 percent of the people identify themselves as Hawai'ian, and 21.4 percent described themselves as mixed. Asians make up the largest group and Caucasians the second

largest. O'ahu, with a population of 900,000, is by far the most populated of the eight main islands.

The state fish is the reef triggerfish, the *humu humu nuku nuku apua'a*—a tongue twister that children love to try to say quickly.

The state flower is the yellow hibiscus; in Hawai'ian, *ma'o hau hele*.

A Few Key Phrases

Learning a few key phrases will help you to enjoy the Hawai'ian culture, especially for hikers asking for directions:

Makai (pronounced ma-KYE)— seaward; *kai* by itself means "sea."

Mauka (MOW-kah, where MOW rhymes with "wow")—toward the mountains

Pali (PAH-lee)—cliff

Pu'u (poo-oo)—hill or mountain top

At Waikīkī:

Diamond Head—toward the east

Ewa (AY-vah)—toward the west

Conversation

Pau (pow)—finished; you may have a waiter say, "all *pau*?"

Hana (hah-nah)—work

Huhu (HOO-hoo)—angry

Aloha (a-LOW-ha)—hello, goodbye, I love you

Mahalo (ma-HA-lo)—thank you

Shaka (shah-kah)—great; your surfing instructor may say this while smiling, extending the little finger and thumb and wiggling his fist.

As you may have noticed, Hawai'ian vowel pronunciation is quite consistent. For *a*, say "ah"; for *e*, "ay"; for i, "ee"; for *o*, "oh"; for *u*, "oo." Combinations are often slurred together; for example, *kai* is pronounced "kye." Note that an *e* at the end of a word is always pronounced. The consonants are pretty much as you are used to, although a *w* in the middle of a word is pronounced "v.")

Hawai'ian words are properly spelled with the addition of two special characters. The *okina* (shown as a single opening quotation mark, ') indicates a glottal stop; uncommon in English, the sound can be heard between the two parts of the expression "uh-oh." The *kahakō* is shown as a short line (macron) above a vowel and indicates a long

(doubled) vowel sound. To enhance your enjoyment of the wonderful Hawai'ian language, these characters are used where possible throughout this guide. However, you may find them omitted on road and trail signs.

Hazards

Hyperthermia (Overheating)

To avoid overheating, you should take these precautions when hiking in Hawai'i:

• Begin your hikes early in the day to avoid the intense midday heat.

• Take a quart of water for each person on the short hikes and two quarts each for the long hikes.

• Drink some water every 20 minutes to keep from becoming dehydrated.

• If you become overheated, take a dip in one of the many streams and pools (do not do so if you have any open cuts or sores—see Leptospirosis, p. 17).

• Wear a lightweight sun hat, preferably the floppy kind that shields your eyes and neck. Wear sunglasses and use sunblock liberally.

Hypothermia (Low Body Temperature)
Despite the warm climate of O'ahu, hypothermia is still possible. Always bring a lightweight rainproof shell and a light wool or polypropylene shirt in case of heavy rainfall or chilling winds.

Extreme Weather Conditions
Check the weather conditions before starting out. Avoid hiking in gullies or stream valleys during torrential rain- storms, and do not hike when there is a hurricane (tropical cyclone) warning. For weather information, call the Nation- al Weather Service at (808) 973-4380.

Narrow Trails
Most of the trails in this book are easy and have few hazards. However, some are along steep ridges. Watch your step and be cautious.

Rockfalls
Rockfalls may occur during or shortly after a heavy rainfall. Be cautious when hiking in gorges, near waterfalls and beneath steep rock faces.

Leptospirosis
Take the following precautions to avoid contracting this bacterial disease, which may produce flulike symptoms in 2–14 days and can result in liver damage and death:

• Never drink stream or lake water unless the water has been boiled or chemically treated.

• Leptospirosis bacteria can enter through the nose, mouth, eyes or cuts and scratches. Be cautious about taking a dip in a stream or lake, and avoid getting stream and lake water splashed on your nose, mouth, eyes or cuts and scratches.

• Wear long pants when hiking through streams to avoid scratches.

Hunters

Several of the hikes in this book are in areas where hunting for pigs, goats or birds occurs. If there is a hunter check-in station at the trailhead, be cautious and stay on the hiking trail, because the hunters usually stay away from the trail. It is a good idea to wear colorful attire for all the hikes—you will be more visible in hunting areas and easier to spot in case of an emergency.

Marijuana Growers

The trails in this book are, for the most part, well traveled and do not cross into areas where there may be marijuana growers. However, hikers are advised to stay on the trails. In the event you do come across an illegal pot patch, leave the area as quickly as possible, because there have been conflicts between hikers and marijuana growers.

Vehicle Break-ins

Never leave valuables in your vehicle when parking at a trailhead. At some trailheads, theft and vandalism are serious problems. These trailheads are noted in the trail descriptions, and alternative parking locations are recommended. Although most of the people of Hawai'i are kind and generous hosts, Hawai'i is experiencing an increasing level of vandalism and crime, often directed at visitors driving rental cars. One local writer advises tourists to leave their rental cars with doors and trunk unlocked and to remove everything from the vehicle if they are parking for a prolonged period in an area of high vandalism. Our own car was broken into at the Waimanalo trailhead (see the Maunawili Demonstration Trail, hike 18). Luckily, we had left nothing in the vehicle.

In Case of Emergency

If possible, bring a cell phone so that you can call 911 for assistance. However, a few areas do not have coverage. If you require rescue, give 911 your location. In an emergency, be visible (wear bright clothing) and be noisy (use a whistle to attract attention). Stay calm, stay put and stay warm.

Final Advice

The condition of trails continually changes. Always use your own judgment regarding the safety of the trail. Remember, Hawai'i is the indigenous land of the Hawai'ian people. Respect their property and their culture. Do not disturb sacred offerings and be respectful when visiting religious sites. Take nothing but photos; leave nothing but footprints.

Maunawili Falls Trail

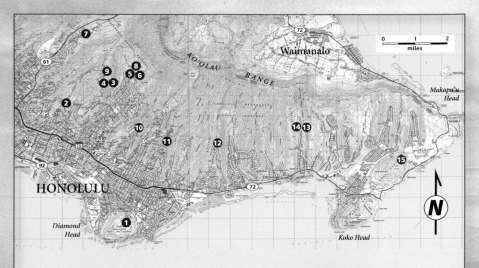

1. Diamond Head

Map: USGS Honolulu

Distance: 1.6 miles out and back

Time: 1.5 hours

Rating: moderate with steep uphill

Elevation gain: 560 feet

Footwear and special equipment: trail shoes, flashlight, hat, water, sunscreen and sunglasses

Best time and season: early morning to avoid hot sun; all seasons

Distance from Waikīkī to trailhead: approx. 4 miles

Fees and hours of operation: $1 fee per hiker and $5 fee per private vehicle; open 6:00 AM to 6:00 PM.

Highlights

This hike from the center of the Diamond Head (Leʻahi) volcanic crater to its highest point (elevation 761 feet) offers a spectacular view of Honolulu (Kuamoʻokāne) and the Koʻolau Range. The World War I and World War II fortifications will be of special interest to military buffs. This trail is a perfect family hike.

Access Map

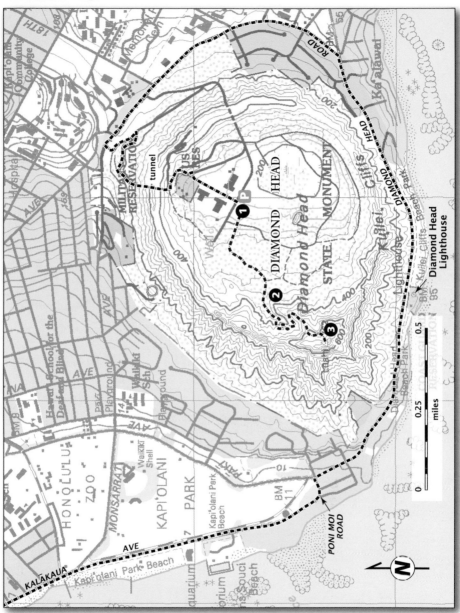

Access from Waikīkī to Trailhead

From downtown Waikīkī, drive, walk, cycle or bus (contact TheBus for details, see p. 12).

Proceed southeast on Kalākaua Avenue, passing the intersection with Monsarrat Avenue, then curve left onto Poni Moi Road. Immediately, turn right onto

Trail Map

MILITARY
RESERVATION

tunnel

US
RES

Well

400

200

P
1

2

DIAMOND   HEAD

Diamond Head

STATE   MONUMENT

762

3

600

400

200

Kuilei   Cliffs

HEAD

Lighthouse

DIAMOND   Beach   Park

GUARD
VATION   BM
95   Diamond Head
Lighthouse

0   0.25
miles

N

Diamond Head Road. Along this scenic oceanside route, you pass Diamond Head Beach and the Diamond Head Lighthouse on your right.

Follow Diamond Head Road as it curves left around the crater, then turn left into the Diamond Head Park entrance (3.4 miles from downtown Waikīkī).

The access road passes through a short tunnel into the crater. There is parking near the trailhead.

Walkers and cyclists should be cautious in the tunnel, because it is quite narrow.

Trail Description

1. From the trailhead, the route passes along the bottom of the crater through a grove of koa haole. Soon the trail becomes steep and somewhat rugged as it fishtails back and forth up the crater rim. Before you reach the first set of stairs, there is a lookout on your left. This foundation held a winch and cable used to lift materials from the crater floor.

View of Waikīkī from the summit.

2. The first set of steep stairs leads into a dark tunnel. The second stairway consists of 99 steps and leads into the second tunnel and then into the spiral staircase. You may need your flashlight here. This section consists of four levels of the Fire Control Station; built between 1908 and 1910, it was once used to plot the direction of artillery fire from several batteries. The observation equipment is still present on the third level.

3. When you reach the top, exit through the slits to the exterior of the crater and take the metal staircase to the observation station, elevation 761 feet. To the east are Koko Head and the ridge of the Ko'olau Range; to the northwest, Waikīkī.

How was Diamond Head Named?

The Hawai'ian name for Diamond Head is Le'ahi. Two explanations for the Hawai'ian name have been offered. According to one of them, Hi'iaka, sister of the fire goddess Pele, gave Le'ahi its name because the summit resembles the *lea* (forehead) of the fish known as '*ahi*. Alternatively, the name may be derived from the Hawai'ian word for "fire headland," referring to the navigational fires that were lit at the summit to assist people traveling along the shoreline by canoe. Le'ahi was renamed "Diamond Head" by Western explorers and traders who visited the site in the late 18th century and thought the calcite crystals in the rocks were diamonds.

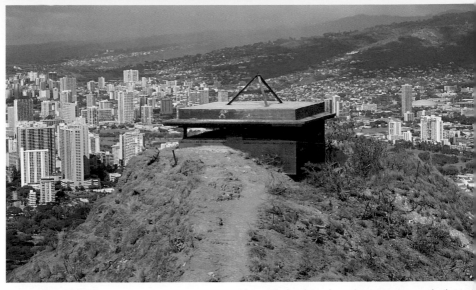

Geological History

Diamond Head was created some 500,000 years ago. Magma ejected during a single but brief eruption, probably lasting several days, was broken down into ash and fine particles by the ocean water and steam. Blown into the air, these particles then cemented together into a rock called tuff, which forms Diamond Head. Koko Head, to the east, was created at about the same time.

Pacific Golden Plover

The winter plumage of this shorebird is fluffy brown, with gold spotting on the back. In winter, adults migrate to Hawai'i from Alaska.

Gray Francolin

This bird is brown overall, with heavy barring across the back and wings, and it has reddish brown legs. The gray francolin is 12 inches in height, and its call is a strident *titur, titur*.

Above: The bunkers along the crater rim were built in 1915. Although the fortification was built to defend O'ahu, no guns were ever fired from Diamond Head, even in the infamous attack on Pearl Harbor in 1941.

Below: Ninety-nine steps up the crater rim.

Plants to Look For

Koa haole

A small, weedy, leguminous tree or shrub from Central America with many uses, koa haole has small, white pompom flowers, feathery compound leaves and large, brown seedpods.

Kiawe (algaroba, mesquite)

Brought to Hawai'i in the 19th century, this medium-sized, thorny, deep-rooted tree has depleted groundwater supplies in many areas. It has ferny branches bearing fernlike leaves and caterpillar-like, yellow flower clusters. The extremely hard wood is popular for woodworking and as a barbecue fuel.

Koa haole (above), Kiawe (below)

2. Makiki Valley Loop
(Kanealole, Makiki Valley and Maunalaha Loop Trail)

Highlights

This pleasant, shady loop trail winds steeply alongside the Kanealole Stream, crosses the Makiki Valley and the Moleka Stream and then drops down to the Hawai'i Nature Center. This hike offers beautiful views of Honolulu and Diamond Head. A rich variety of trees and plants grows in this

Map: USGS Honolulu

Distance: 2.5 mile loop

Time: 3 hours

Rating: moderate

Elevation gain: 800 feet

Footwear and special equipment: trail shoes

Best time and season: all seasons; may be slippery when raining

Distance from Waikīkī to trailhead: approx. 3.5 miles; the road into the Hawai'i Nature Center closes at 6:00 PM.

Access Map

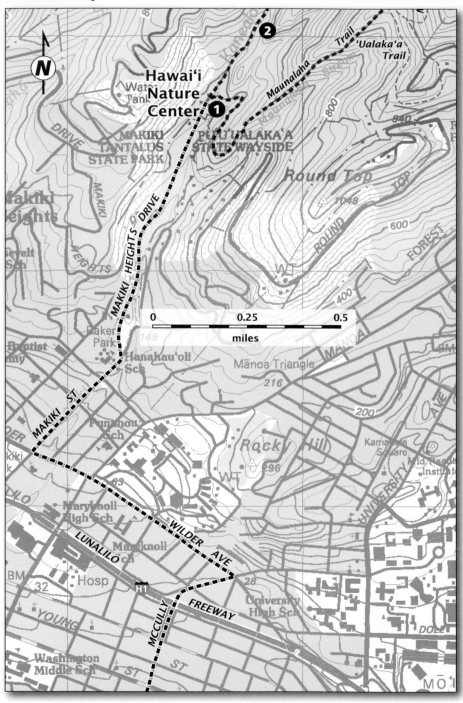

mixed forest with its moderate rainfall. A visit to the Hawai'i Nature Center, where you can pick up trail maps and learn about O'ahu's natural history, is highly recommended.

Access from Waikīkī to Trailhead

Take McCully Street *mauka* (toward the mountains) across the Lunalilo Freeway (H-1), curve right as it becomes Metcalf Street and continue for one block. Go sharply left onto Wilder Avenue. Pass Punahou Street, continue for two blocks and go right on Makiki Street.

Follow Makiki Street to a Y-intersection, where you go left on Makiki Heights Drive. Continue until you reach a left hairpin turn and take the signed road to the Hawai'i Nature Center. Park at the bottom gate in the designated hiker parking area.

Trail Map

Trail Description

1. Follow the Makiki Arboretum Trail from the parking lot to the restrooms. This arboretum features a two-acre native garden (all plants are indigenous). Near the restrooms, look for the Maunalaha Trail sign and follow the trail for 300 feet to a junction with a bench, where you go left onto the Kanealole Trail. You will return on the right fork, the Maunalaha Trail.

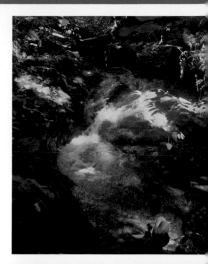

2. Your route follows the Kanealole Stream. There is a tiny waterfall to your right, about 20 feet off the trail.

3. At the intersection, turn right onto the Makiki Valley Trail. The trail crosses the Kanealole Stream and then winds up and down the gullies.

4. Cross a bridge over the Moleka Stream before ascending a long series of steps.

5. Reach the well-marked four-way junction with the Makiki Valley, 'Ualaka'a and Maunalaha trails. Go right onto the Maunalaha Trail, which takes you back to the Hawai'i Nature Center.

Plants to Look For

Ki (ti)

The ki (pronounced "kee") plant was brought here by the Polynesians in the fourth century AD, when these seagoing people first arrived on the islands. It is a small, green shrub with a spray of long leaves reaching up to 12 feet in the air. Hawai'ians use the leaves, called *luau*, to wrap food for cooking. In earlier days, the plant was used to make a weak alcoholic drink, to thatch dwellings, to make rain capes and for ceremonial purposes. The plant is believed to protect the Hawai'ians' dwellings, and it is sometimes still seen as a hedge surrounding modern dwellings. In ancient times, stone houses would be surrounded by ki plants. Present-day archaeologists search for concentrations of ki plants as a means of locating ancient Polynesian dwellings.

3. Moleka and 'Ualaka'a Trails

Highlights

Just minutes away from the crowded tourist center of Honolulu, these trails nevertheless offer the peace and beauty of the tropical forest. The views from Round Top Drive on your way to the trailhead are spectacular. Watch for a variety of plant and bird life as well.

Map: USGS Honolulu

Distance: 1.3 miles round trip

Time: 1 hour

Rating: easy

Elevation gain: 350 feet

Footwear and special equipment: trail shoes

Best time and season: all seasons

Distance from Waikīkī to trailhead: approx. 7 miles

Access Map

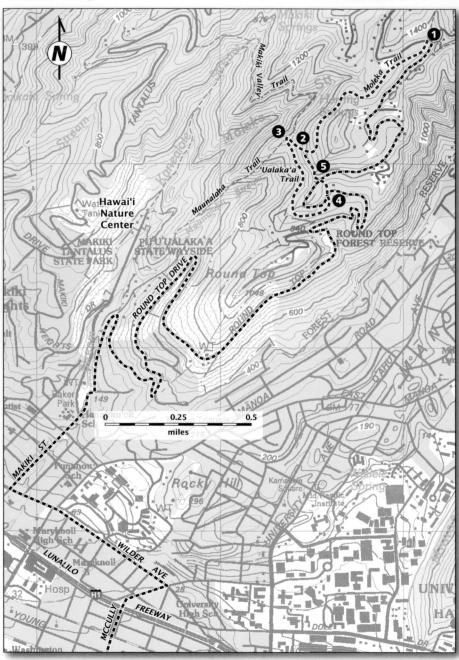

Access from Waikīkī to Trailhead

Take McCully Street *mauka* (toward the mountains) across the Lunalilo Freeway (H-1), curve right as it becomes Metcalf Street and continue for one block. Turn sharply left onto Wilder Avenue.

Pass Punahou Street, continue for two blocks and go right onto Makiki Street. Ascend on Makiki for four blocks till you reach a fork, then bear right (the left fork is Makiki Heights). Soon Makiki turns into Round Top Drive.

Follow the switchbacking Round Top Drive for 4.3 miles. Park on the left at the trailhead for Moleka and Mānoa Cliff trails.

Trail Map

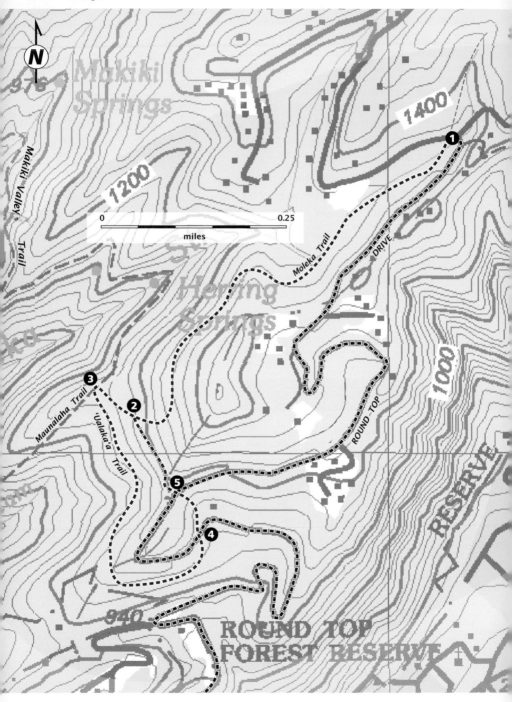

Trail Description

1. The Moleka Trail descends from Round Top Drive over wooden steps on a well-maintained trail, then begins a steep switchback before reaching a T-junction.

2. Turn right onto the Makiki Valley Trail to begin the 'Ualaka'a loop trail. At the end of the loop, you will return on the trail to your left.

3. Soon you reach a four-way junction marked by a trail map and a bench. At this junction, the Makiki Valley Trail intersects with the 'Ualaka'a Trail (the route you are taking) and the Maunalaha Trail, which descends to the Hawai'i Nature Center. Take the 'Ualaka'a Trail (the fork to the left).

4. Where the trail intersects Round Top Drive, cross the paved road and reenter the forest, picking up the trail on the other side. Continue on the 'Ualaka'a Trail as it zigzags upward to meet Round Top Drive again.

5. Cross Round Top Drive again and walk about 150 feet up the road to where the trail marked Makiki Valley reenters the forest. It is a short distance to the T-junction where you close the loop. Return on the Moleka Trail, which ascends to the trailhead and parking area.

Lucia Chang (above) guides visitors on the Makiki Valley Trails. She sang a Hawaiian love song to us when we met on the trail.

4. Mānoa Cliff Loop
(Moleka, Makiki Valley, Kalawahine and Nahuina Trails)

Map: USGS Honolulu

Distance: 6 mile loop

Time: 5 hours

Rating: moderate

Elevation gain: 880 feet

Footwear and special equipment: trail shoes

Best time and season: all seasons

Distance from Waikīkī to trailhead: approx. 7 miles

Highlights

This combination of the Moleka, Makiki Valley, Nahuina and Kalawahine trails turns these short, out-and-back hikes into an enjoyable loop trail that includes the spectacular yet less frequently used Mānoa Cliff Trail.

Access Map

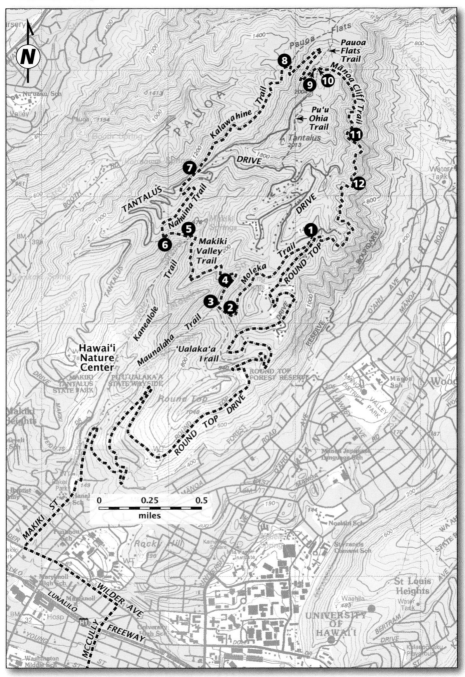

Trail Map

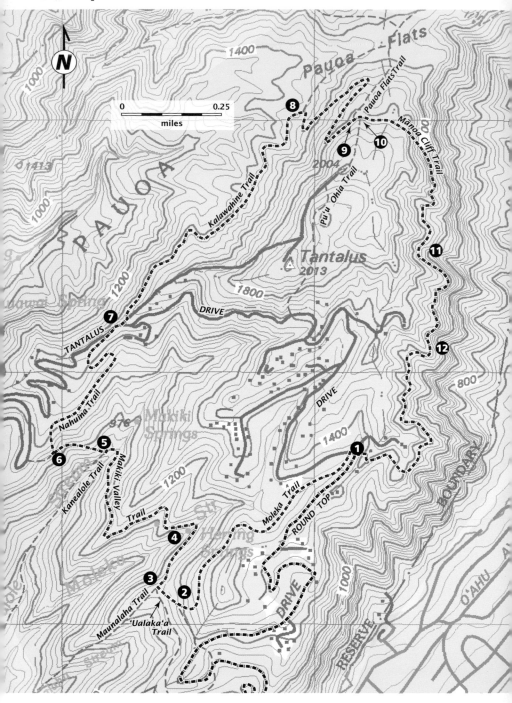

Access from Waikīkī to Trailhead

Take McCully Street *mauka* (toward the mountains) across the Lunalilo Freeway (H-1), curve right as it becomes Metcalf Street and continue for one block. Go sharply left onto Wilder Avenue.

Pass Punahou Street, continue for two blocks and go right on Makiki Street. Ascend on Makiki for four blocks till you reach a fork, then bear right. Soon Makiki turns into Round Top Drive.

Follow the switchbacking Round Top Drive for 4.3 miles. Park on the left at the trailhead for the Moleka and Mānoa Cliff trails.

Trail Description

1. The Moleka Trail descends from Round Top Drive down steps on a well-maintained trail, then ascends a steep switchback.

2. When you reach the T-junction, go right onto the Makiki Valley Trail.

3. Soon you reach a four-way junction marked by a trail map and a bench. At this junction, the Makiki Valley Trail intersects with the Maunalaha Trail, which descends to the Hawai'i Nature Center and the 'Ualaka'a Trail. Continue to the right on the Makiki Valley Trail.

4. After crossing the Moleka Stream, you come to a spot with a great view of Honolulu and the Pacific Ocean.

5. The trail crosses two more bridges before intersecting with the Kanealole Trail, which goes down to the Hawai'i Nature Center. Take the right fork, which ascends steeply.

6. Soon you arrive at a T-junction; go right up the switchbacks of the Nahuina Trail.

7. Intersect with Tantalus Drive on what local residents call the "Hogback." Go right on Tantalus Drive approximately 0.2 miles until you see the Kalawahine trailhead on your left, on the *mauka* (mountain) side of Tantalus. Take this trail.

The sign indicates both the Kalawahine and Mānoa Cliff trails; the Kalawahine Trail is shown as Mānoa Cliff Trail on some maps.

8. When you reach a T-junction, stay right on what is now the Mānoa Cliff Trail. The trail to the left is a continuation of the Kalawahine.

9. At the next T-junction, this time with the Pauoa Flats Trail, keep right to stay on the Mānoa Cliff Trail. This section can be muddy in wet weather, but it is nevertheless interesting because of the wild ginger plants, which area residents sometimes gather.

10. A short distance farther, at the T-junction with the Puʻu Ohia Trail, stay left on the Mānoa Cliff Trail.

11. Follow the ridge overlooking the Mānoa Valley, with a distant view of Mānoa Falls. The trail narrows in places.

12. Look for several plant interpretive signs along this section. After passing a bench, you come to a spot where you have a view of Diamond Head. Complete the loop when you come out on Round Top Drive just opposite the Moleka trailhead, where you began the hike.

Plants to Look For

Ginger

Familiar as an ingredient in Asian cooking and ginger snaps, ginger produces upright shoots that sprout up from rhizomes at the base of the plant. The knobby and fleshy rhizomes are covered by ringlike scars. When handled, the leaves, which are reminiscent of bamboo, release a gingery odor. During the flowering season, the plants produce reddish purple blooms with a cream-blotched base. Ginger can grow to 3 feet tall. However, because the local people often cut the plants along this trail to use the rhizomes for cooking, they seldom reach that height.

Ginger (this page)

5. Mānoa Falls

Map: USGS Honolulu

Distance: 1.6 miles out and back

Time: 1.5 hours

Rating: easy

Elevation gain: 600 feet

Footwear and special equipment: walking shoes

Best time and season: early morning, to avoid heavy usage at peak times; the falls are more spectacular after rainfall, but heavy downpours have caused rockfalls, so be careful; trail may be closed because of heavy rain

Distance from Waikīkī to trailhead: approx. 3 miles

Highlights

Mānoa ("vast") Falls is the best known and most frequently visited waterfall on Oʻahu. It can be spectacular during or after a rainfall.

Access from Waikīkī to Trailhead

Note that the trialhead area is known for theft and

Access Map

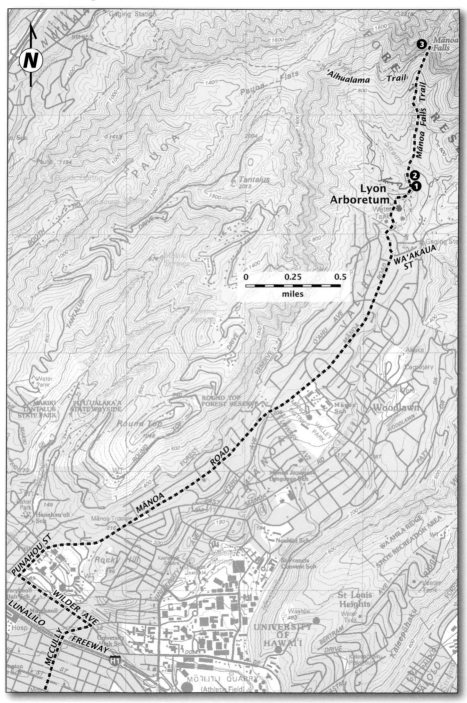

Trail Map

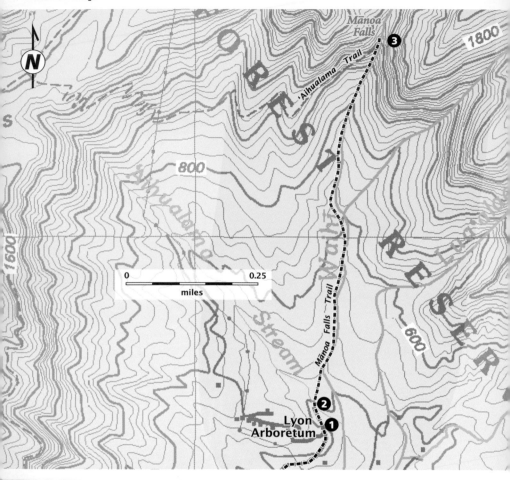

vandalism, so taking the bus (see p. 12) is an especially attractive alternative to driving.

Take McCully Street *mauka* (toward the mountains) across the Lunalilo Freeway (H-1), curve right as it becomes Metcalf Street and continue for one block. Go sharply left onto Wilder Avenue.

Proceed seven blocks and turn right on Punahou Street. Continue as it becomes Mānoa Road. At the Y-junction with East Mānoa, stay left. At a four-way stop, continue straight ahead on Mānoa (left is Oʻahu Avenue, Pawaina Street is right).

When you reach the intersection with Waʻakaua (on the right), you can leave your car and walk 0.5 miles to the trailhead. Alternatively, continue to a paid parking lot, where an attendant will look after your vehicle for $5.

Trail Description

1. Pass the access road, on the left, to Lyon Arboretum, a feature worth visiting after the hike. The trail to Mānoa Falls begins after a barrier and narrows to a small, sometimes rough path.

2. The route crosses the ʻAihualama Stream on a bridge and then goes alongside the Waihī ("trickling water") Stream past tangled hau trees.

3. When you reach the T-junction with the ʻAihualama Trail on your left, stay right on the wider Mānoa Trail. You shortly reach the falls, where there are benches. The beauty of the falls varies, depending on the season. In dry weather, there may be only a trickle. During very heavy rains, it is dangerous to stand under the falls, because rocks and debris are sometimes pushed over the lip, and the entire trail to the falls may be closed at such times. For safety reasons, taking a dip in the pool at the base of the falls is no longer permitted. If you swim in the streams or pools of Hawaiʻi, take precautions against contacting leptospirosis (see p. 17). When you are finished enjoying the falls, retrace your steps to the trailhead.

6. 'Aihualama to Nu'uanu Overlook

Map: USGS Honolulu

Distance: 3.2 miles out and back

Time: 2 hours

Rating: moderate (one steep, rocky section)

Elevation gain: 1200 feet

Footwear and special equipment: trail shoes

Best time and season: morning, to avoid the crowds; all seasons; slippery in heavy rain

Distance from Waikīkī to trailhead: approx. 3 miles

Highlights

This short hike features a variety of trees and terrain. As well, it rewards with a lookout over the Nu'unau Valley, with views of the windward side of the island.

Access from Waikīkī to Trailhead

Note that this hike begins on the Mānoa Falls Trail

Access Map

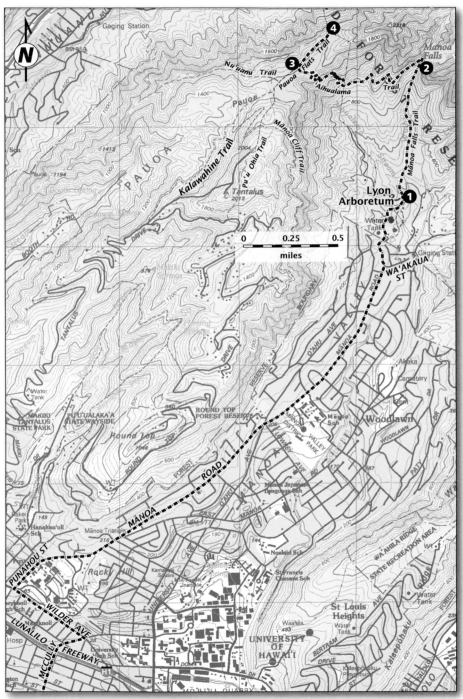

Trail Map

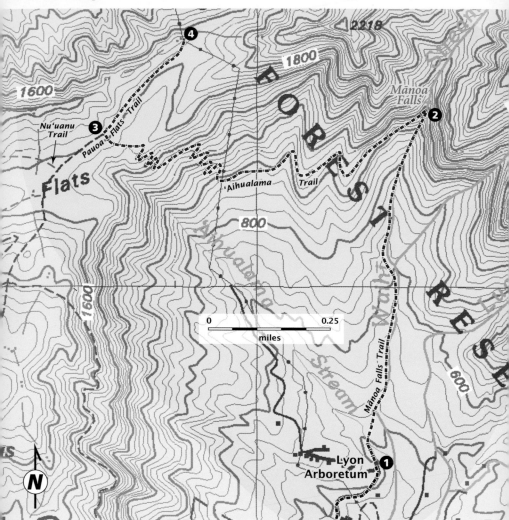

and turns off just before the falls. Because the trailhead area is known for theft and vandalism, taking the bus (see p. 12) is an especially attractive alternative to driving.

In wet weather, use caution on the slippery sections of a steep incline on the 'Aihualama Trail.

Take McCully Street *mauka* (toward the mountains) across the Lunalilo Freeway (H-1), curve right as it becomes Metcalf Street and continue for one block. Turn sharply left onto Wilder Avenue.

Proceed seven blocks and turn right onto Punahou Street. Continue as it becomes Mānoa Road. At the Y-junction with East Mānoa, stay left. At a four-way stop, continue straight ahead on Mānoa (left is O'ahu Avenue, Pawaina Street is right).

When you reach the intersection with Wa'akaua (on the right), you can leave your car and walk 0.5 miles to the trailhead. Alternatively, continue to a paid parking lot, where an attendant will look after your vehicle for $5.

Trail Description

1. Pass the access to Lyon Arboretum on the left and look for the trailhead for Mānoa Falls. The trail to Mānoa Falls begins after a barrier and narrows to a small, sometimes rough path. The trail to Mānoa Falls is well defined (see hike 5).

2. Just before you reach the falls, take the signed 'Aihualama Trail on your left. (The falls are well worth a visit if you have not yet seen them.) The trail ascends over very rough, rocky terrain before reaching a grove of bamboo trees. A few minutes out, you get views of Mānoa Valley and a glimpse of Diamond Head, after which you pass through a forest affected by a plant parasite that leaves the trees looking denuded and appearing to be dying. This area can be slippery during heavy rain. The trail winds up switchbacks and then passes through another section of bamboo trees before descending to a trail junction.

3. Turn right onto the Pauoa Flats Trail, which may be unmarked.

4. Continue until you reach the Nu'uanu Overlook. Below are views of the Pali Highway, the ocean and the town of Kailua on the windward side of the island. Return via the same route.

7. Judd Memorial Trail and Jackass Ginger Pool

Map: USGS Honolulu

Distance: 1 mile loop

Time: 2 hours

Rating: easy, but with two stream crossings on boulders

Elevation gain: 250 feet

Footwear and special equipment: trail shoes

Best time and season: any, although the trail down to the pool might be slippery in rainy weather

Distance to trailhead: approx. 8 miles

Highlights

Deep, cool Jackass Ginger Pool is not to be missed. This swimming hole is a popular spot for local residents. At one time, Hawai'ian royalty would sit on ti leaves and slide on the mud down the steep banks into the pool.

Access Map

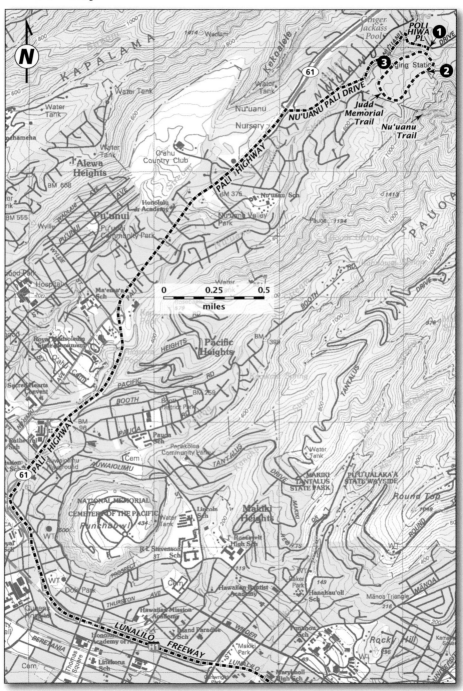

Trail Map

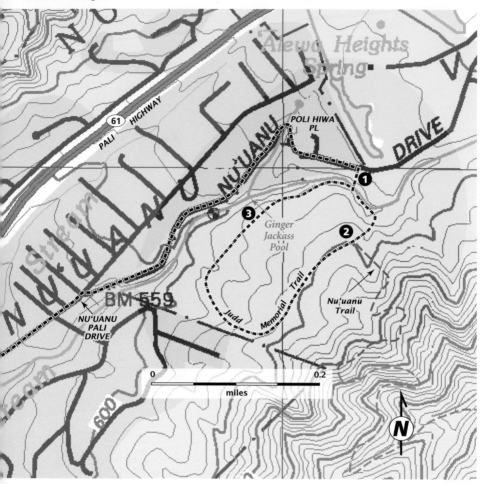

Access from Waikīkī to Trailhead

Take McCully Street *mauka* (toward the mountains) across the Lunalilo Freeway (H-1) and go left onto the H-1 westbound. From the H-1, turn right onto the Pali Highway (SR 61) at exit 21B. Drive 2.7 miles along the Pali Highway and turn right onto Nuʻuanu Pali Drive. There is a health center in a large, white building on the left corner of this intersection just after you turn.

Drive 0.3 miles and stay right when Nuʻuanu Pali Drive forks right at Old Pali Road. You soon cross a stone bridge and pass Polihiwa Place on the left.

About 0.8 miles from the fork, look for several concrete barriers just before a second bridge.

Immediately after crossing the bridge, park on the side of the road. Look for the poorly marked trailhead on your right.

Trail Description

1. From the small trailhead sign, walk through an open area toward the stream. Use caution when crossing the stream on the boulders—it can be tricky in high water; a trekking pole or sturdy stick can help with balance. Once across, do not take the spur trail that goes downstream. Yellow arrows mark the Judd Memorial Trail, but be careful not to accidentally take one of the spur trails that go off it. The trail begins in a bamboo grove, where there is a signposted fork in the trail. Take the left fork (the right fork is the return trail).

2. The trail passes through a grove of Cook pines, and soon you reach the junction with the Nuʻuanu Trail. Stay right on the Judd Memorial Trail.

3. The trail passes above the Nuʻuanu Stream. Jackass Ginger Pool can be seen below. Be careful

Charles S. Judd

The trail and the Charles S. Judd Memorial Grove are named after the territorial forester for Hawaiʻi, who held the position from 1915 to 1939. Born in Hawaiʻi, he graduated from the Yale Forestry School. Although he planted these exotic Cook pines, he also spoke out for the protection of native forest from invasive species when the military cut new roads. He was also keenly aware of the role that forests play in watershed management.

as you descend to the pool, because the trails down to the pool are precipitous. You can enjoy a cooling swim if you have no open cuts, because leptospirosis is a risk (see p. 17). Local residents sometimes swing from ropes here and jump into the deep pool, but it is dangerous to dive into. When you are done here, clamber up the bank to the loop trail and turn left, heading upstream. Do your best to stay on the main trail and avoid the several new makeshift trails. However, all the trails heading upstream eventually lead to the end of the loop. When you close the loop, turn left and—with care—recross the stream to the trailhead.

Nu'uana Stream—cross with caution, especially in high water.

Plants to Look For

Christmas berry (p. 190), Cook pine

Cook pine

The Cook pine, which is native to New Caledonia in the South Pacific, is recognizable by its beautiful symmetric form. The short needles might be said to make each branch resemble a batch of coarse, green pipecleaners. When first introduced to Hawai'i, this tall tree was incorrectly identified as the closely related Norfolk Island pine; it is also related to the monkey puzzle. Because of its attractive grain, the wood is popular for woodworking.

Cook pine (above), Christmas berry (below)

8. 'Aihualama to Judd Memorial Trail

Map: USGS Honolulu

Distance: 4.3 miles one way (arrange for transportation at Judd Memorial Trailhead)

Time: 2.5 hours

Rating: moderate (one steep, rocky section on the ascent; one stream crossing on boulders)

Elevation gain: 1200 feet

Footwear and special equipment: trail shoes

Best time and season: morning, to avoid the crowds; all seasons; may be slippery in the rain

Distance from Waikīkī to trailhead: approx. 3 miles

Highlights

This trail passes through the densest bamboo grove of any of the hiking trails in this guide. As well, it offers amazing views where it crosses over two ridges.

Access from Waikīkī to Judd Memorial Trail

(where you drop off a vehicle or arrange for transportation)

Access Map

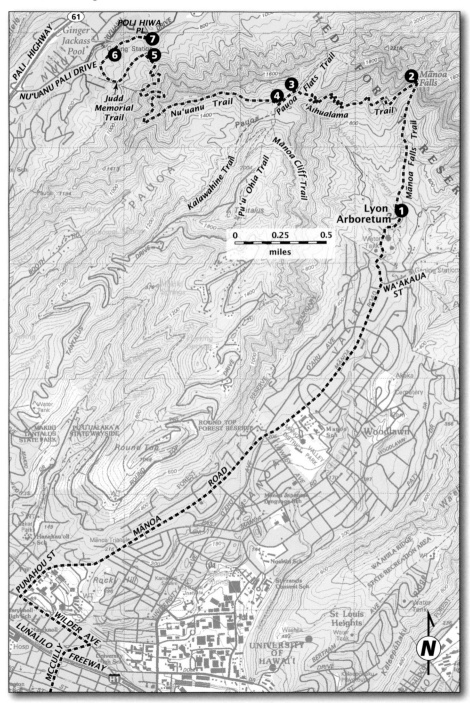

Trail Map

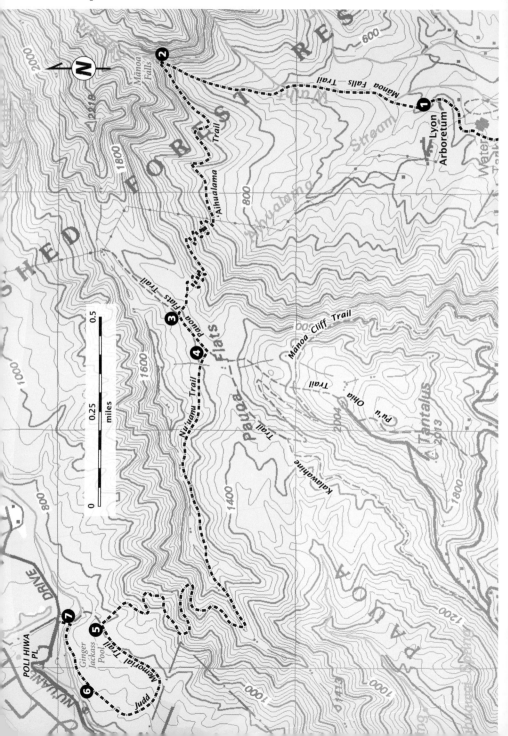

Note that this hike begins on the Mānoa Falls Trail and turns off just before the falls. In wet weather, use caution on the slippery sections of a steep incline on the 'Aihualama Trail.

I prefer this route as a one-way hike from the Mānoa Falls trail over to the Nu'uanu Valley. However, it does require making arrangements to drop off a vehicle or to be picked up at the Judd Memorial trailhead. Alternatively, it is possible to take a bus to the Mānoa Falls trailhead and to catch a bus on Nu'uanu Pali Drive. Pick up a bus schedule from TheBus or write TheBus (see p. 12), enclosing a stamped self-addressed envelope, for a free schedule.

To drop off a car or get picked up at the end of your hike, use the following directions. (For a map of the access, see hike 7, Judd Memorial Trail and Jackass Ginger Pool.)

Take McCully Street *mauka* (toward the mountains) across the Lunalilo Freeway (H-1) and go left onto the H-1 west-bound. From the H-1, turn right onto the Pali Highway (SR 61) at exit 21B and continue on the Pali Highway for 2.7 miles, turning right onto Nu'uanu Pali Drive. There is a health center in a large, white building on the left corner of this intersection just after you turn.

Drive 0.3 miles and stay right when Nu'uanu Pali Drive forks right at Old Pali Road. You soon cross a stone bridge and pass Poli Hiwa Place on the left.

About 0.8 miles from the fork, look for several concrete barriers just before a second bridge.

Immediately after crossing the bridge, park on the side of the road. Look for the poorly marked trailhead on your right.

Access from Waikīkī to Trailhead

Note that the trialhead area is known for theft and vandalism, so taking the bus (see p. 12) is an especially attractive alternative to driving.

Take McCully Street *mauka* (toward the mountains) across the Lunalilo Freeway (H-1), curve right as it becomes Metcalf Street and continue for one block. Turn sharply left onto Wilder Avenue.

Proceed seven blocks and turn right onto Punahou Street. Continue as it becomes Mānoa Road. At the Y-junction with East Mānoa, stay left. At a four-way stop, continue straight ahead on Mānoa (left is O'ahu Avenue, Pawaina Street is right).

When you reach the intersection with Wa'akaua (on the right), you can leave your car and walk 0.5 miles to the trailhead. Alternatively, continue to a paid parking lot, where an attendant will look after your vehicle for $5.

Trail Description

1. To begin the 'Aihualama ("eat lama fruit") Trail, first hike toward Mānoa Falls, passing the roadway into the Lyon Arboretum on your left. The trail to Mānoa Falls begins after a barrier and narrows to a small, sometimes rough, path (see hike 5). The portion of this hike on the Mānoa Trail is heavily used, so begin early in the day.

2. The well-marked 'Aihualama Trail is on your left just before you reach the falls. Take time to visit the spectacular Mānoa Falls before continuing. The 'Aihualama Trail begins over very rough, rocky terrain as it ascends the first ridge. A few minutes out, you get views of Mānoa Valley and a glimpse of Diamond Head. You then pass through a forest affected by a plant parasite that leaves the trees looking denuded and appearing to be dying. This area can be slippery during heavy rain. The trail winds up switchbacks and reaches another section of bamboo trees before descending to a trail junction.

3. Turn left onto the Pauoa Flats Trail, which may be unmarked.

4. In a few minutes, you reach the junction where you turn right onto the Nu'uanu Trail. Continue on this trail for 1.5 miles, eventually descending the ridge into the Nu'uanu Valley. Avoid the many shortcuts as you descend because these trails are causing erosion.

5. When you get to the intersection with the Judd Memorial Trail, take the left fork through this beautiful forest of Cook pines. (A right turn would take you to the hike's end in just a few minutes, but you would miss seeing Jackass Ginger Pool.)

6. In about 15 to 20 minutes, listen for the sound of the Nu'uanu Stream and then look for an indistinct foot trail to your left to take you down a steep slope to Jackass Ginger Pool. After visiting the pool, do your best to stay on the main trail and avoid the several new makeshift trails. However, all the trails heading upstream eventually lead to the end of the loop. Turn left when you reach a crossing point in the stream.

7. Cross the stream on boulders, taking care, especially in high water. A trekking pole or sturdy stick can help with support as you move from rock to rock. Pick up your car or meet up with your ride at the parking lot on Nu'uanu Pali. Alternatively, check your bus schedule and take TheBus.

9. Pu'u Ohia & Pauoa Flats to Nu'uanu Lookout

Map: USGS Honolulu

Distance: 3 miles

Time: 3 hours

Rating: moderate

Elevation gain: 100 feet

Footwear and special equipment: light hiking boots

Best time and season: all seasons

Distance from Waikīkī to trailhead: approx. 7 miles

Highlights

This hike is a true tropical forest walk over roots and through bamboo groves. The difficult trail conditions are balanced by the beautiful view of windward O'ahu.

Access Map

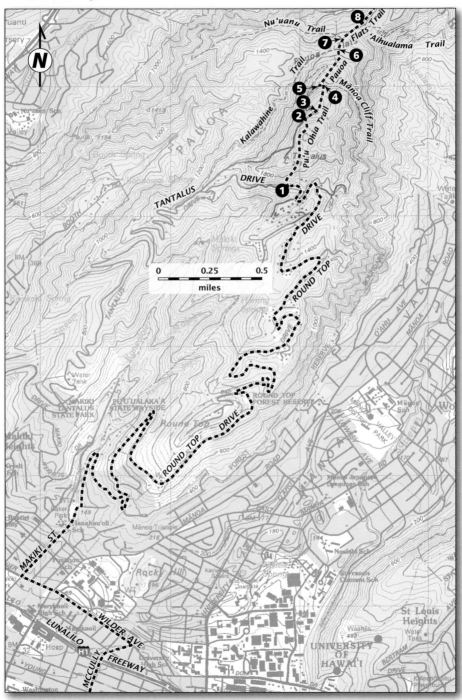

Trail Map

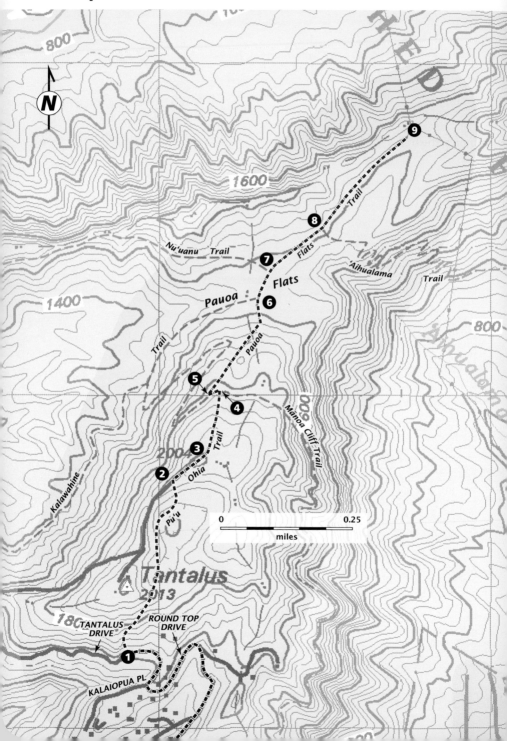

Access from Waikīkī to Trailhead

Take McCully Street *mauka* (toward the mountains) across the Lunalilo Freeway (H-1), curve right as it becomes Metcalf Street and continue for one block. Go sharply left onto Wilder Avenue.

Pass Punahou Street, continue for two blocks and turn right onto Makiki Street. Ascend on Makiki for four blocks till you reach a fork, then bear right (the left fork is Makiki Heights). Soon Makiki turns into Round Top Drive.

Follow the switchbacking Round Top Drive for 4.3 miles, where you pass the trailhead for Moleka and Mānoa Cliff trails, then continue along Round Top Drive for about another 1.5 miles until you reach the Pu'u Ohia trailhead on your right. There is a parking area on the left. Take all valuables from your vehicle, because some theft and vandalism has occurred at this site.

Trail Description

1. The trail begins on a narrow, ascending path. Stay on the main path and ignore the spur trails through the bamboo. Ascend on steps, staying to your right and ignoring a spur trail.

2. Emerge onto an asphalt service road, where there is a trail sign. Go right and continue on the asphalt road until you reach a large building containing a telephone relay station.

3. Look for the marked trail to the left of the facility and continue on this small forest trail.

4. At the T-junction with the Mānoa Cliff Trail, go left onto Mānoa Cliff Trail for a short distance.

5. Go right onto the Pauoa Flats Trail, first on a rocky path and then on a wide trail with entangled roots—it's not easy walking in this section.

6. At the T-junction with the Kalawahine Trail, go right, staying on the Pauoa Flats Trail.

7. At the junction with the Nu'uanu Trail, stay right and on the main trail as you proceed, avoiding spur trails through the bamboo grove.

8. Upon reaching the junction with the 'Aihualama Trail, stay left and continue until you reach the Nu'uanu Lookout.

9. From this viewpoint, you can see the Pali Highway and a water reservoir down below, along with a view of the Ko'olau Range. Retrace your steps back to the trailhead.

Plants to Look For

Common bamboo

A robust member of the grass family that is easily recognized by its stems, common bamboo is used for fiber and for building materials. It is not indigenous to Hawai'i but is now one of the most prolific plants in the secondary forest.

10. Wa'ahila Ridge

Highlights

The trail is located in the Wa'ahila Ridge State Recreation Area. This shady trail goes along the ridge separating Mānoa and Palolo valleys with breathtaking views on both sides of the ridge.

Map: USGS Honolulu

Distance: 2.8 miles out and back

Time: 2.5 hours

Rating: moderate (one steep boulder climb)

Elevation gain: 900 feet

Footwear and special equipment: trail shoes

Best time and season: all seasons, although the path may be slippery in the rain

Distance from Waikīkī to the trailhead: approx. 4 miles

Access Map

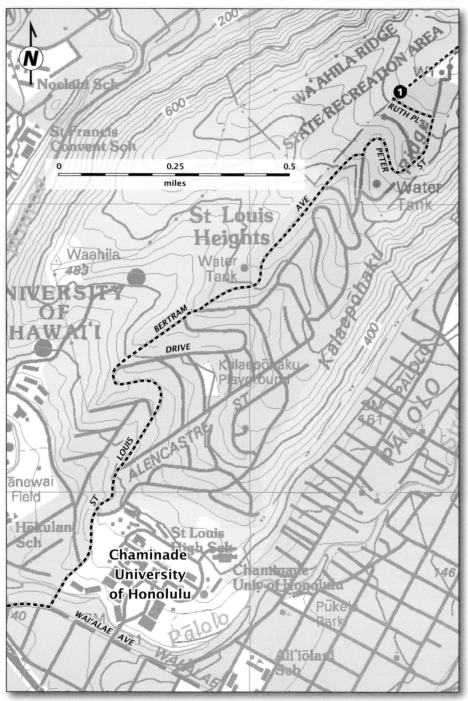

Access from Waikīkī to Trailhead

Take McCully Street *mauka* (toward the mountains) across Ala Wai Canal.

Almost immediately, turn right on Kapiʻolani Boulevard and continue 1.6 miles to the underpass where you cross under the Lunalilo Freeway (H-1). Be careful to stay on Kapiʻolani underneath the freeway and not take an exit onto the freeway. Kapiʻolani soon becomes Waiʻalae Avenue.

About 0.2 miles past the underpass, turn left onto St. Louis Drive. Chaminade University of Honolulu is visible on your right after the turn.

Stay on St. Louis Drive as it curves upward for 0.9 miles to a Y-intersection, where you fork left onto Bertram Street.

Just after Bertram rejoins St. Louis, keep slightly left again to get back onto Bertram. Stay on Bertram until it ends at Peter Street, where you go left.

Pass Quincy Place and then turn left onto Ruth Place and into the Waʻahila Ridge State Recreation Area, where there is a parking area near the trailhead.

Trail Map

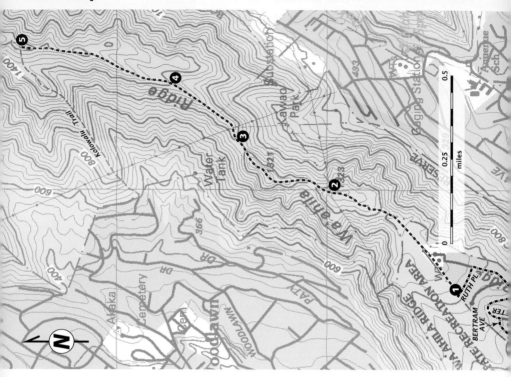

Trail Description

1. The hike begins on a paved trail that soon turns into a dirt path. The first section is rough, with a tangle of roots on the surface.

2. You soon pass under a power line. Stay on the ridge and ignore the spur trails that branch off it. To your right is the community of Pālolo, and to the left is Woodlawn.

3. About 0.6 miles from the trailhead, you reach a short but steep section of boulders. Climb with caution, especially in wet conditions. The scramble is just 10–12 feet high, so it does not constitute a serious difficulty. You pass under the power line again.

4. Watch for a grassy spot with spectacular views of Honolulu, Diamond Head and the Mānoa Valley—a great place for a lunch break.

5. Continue along the undulating ridge until you reach a fork in the trail and the sign for the Kolowalu Trail, which heads down into the Mānoa Valley and the small community of Woodlawn. Turn around here and retrace your steps back to the parking lot.

Plants to Look For

Cook pine (p. 57), ironwood (p. 89), koa haole (p. 26), silk oak, strawberry guava (p. 190), ohi'a 'ai and Christmas berry (p. 190)

Silk oak

This widespread, invasive, fast-growing, medium-sized tree from Australia features brushy, orange flowers (from spring to fall) and fernlike leaves. Cultivated as an ornamental for shade and for its wood, it is not a true oak.

'Ohi'a 'ai (mountain apple)

A medium-sized tree brought by the Polynesians, the 'ohi'a 'ai prefers shaded valleys. It features bright red, shaving-brush flowers in early spring and produces small, apple-like fruits that Hawai'ians use as food and medicinally. This tree is different than the very variable and adaptable 'ōhi'a lehua, with somewhat similar flowers and grayer leaves. The state's most plentiful endemic forest plant, 'ōhi'a lehua has a rich tradition in Hawai'ian legend and uses.

Silk oak (above), 'Ohi'a 'ai (below)

11. Lanipo Mau'umae

Map: USGS Honolulu

Distance: 5 miles out and back

Time: 3 hours

Rating: challenging, with a narrow and steep ridge walk

Elevation gain: 1100 feet

Footwear and special equipment: light hiking boots and binoculars

Best time and season: all seasons; may be slippery when wet

Distance from Waikīkī to trailhead: approx. 6 miles

Highlights

This ridge walk, though very narrow and steep at times, offers excellent views, including a distant view of a little-known crater with a cascading waterfall.

Access from Waikīkī to Trailhead

Take McCully Street *mauka* (toward the mountains)

Access Map

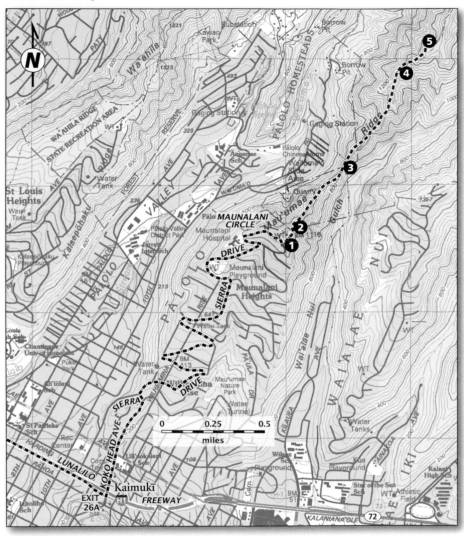

across the Ala Wai Canal and continue eight blocks, turning right (east) on South King Street. Just before reaching the Lunalilo Freeway (H-1), turn left onto Wai'alae Avenue briefly, then take the H-1 entrance ramp on the right, merging onto the H-1 eastbound. From the entrance to H-1 east, drive 1.1 miles and take the Koko Head Avenue exit (26A) in the Kaimukī residential area.

At the top of the off ramp, go left on Koko Head Avenue.

After three blocks, you cross Wai'alae Avenue. Stay on Koko Head Avenue until it ends at Sierra Drive, where you turn right.

Trail Map

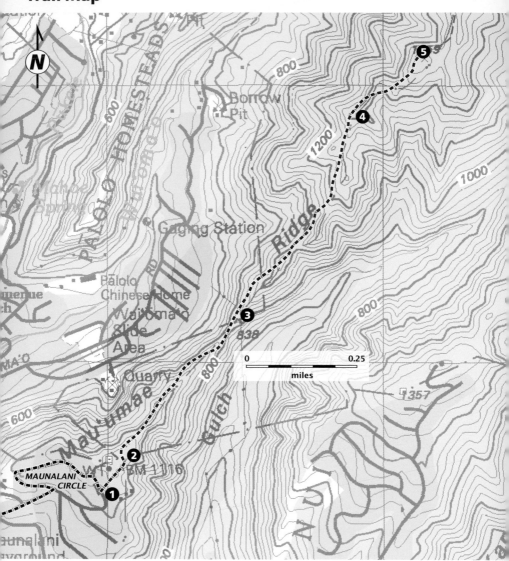

When driving to this trailhead, you continue up the ridge to the limits of the residential development. The many intersecting streets are not all signed. If you get off Sierra Drive, ask for directions or consult your map (if you have one) and get back on Sierra Drive as it ascends the hillside.

Continue up switchbacks, ignoring all turns to stay on Sierra Drive, passing Maunalani Playground on your right and then the Maunalani Nursing Station on your left, until Sierra Drive intersects with Maunalani Circle. Turn left on the circle and, about halfway around the circle, look for a chain-link fence on your left

that surrounds the Board of Water Supply Tank.
Park near the fence. At the corner of the fence,
look for a trail sign for Mau'umae Ridge, across the
street from 4970 Maunalani Circle.

Trail Description

1. The Lanipo Mau'umae ("wilted grass") hike
begins where the chain-link fence ends and the
wooden fence begins. At first, the path is narrow
and covered with roots. In a few minutes, the trail
opens up to a view of the ocean and surrounding
mountain ridges.

2. You quickly reach a spur trail, where you stay
right on the main trail. Soon you reach an excellent
viewpoint. Descend along the ridge with a view of
the residential area to your left, passing a solitary
Formosa koa tree.

3. Ascend on the ridge and go under a power line. The trail is at times rocky and steep as it dips and climbs along the ridge.

4. When you reach an eroded area where the trail is indistinct, the easier route is to the right.

5. The recommended turnaround point of this hike is marked by a grassy knoll with three Cook pines silhouetted against the sky. At this spot, look to your left (north) across the valley to the Ka'au Crater, where a waterfall cascades down from the rim. At this writing, from this point the trail became quite overgrown and unpleasant to walk through. If you decide to continue, the indistinct trail eventually ascends to the summit of Kainawa'aunui.

Plants to Look For

Formosa koa, koa haole (p. 26) and kiawe (p. 26)

Formosa koa (not pictured)
This invasive tree from the Phillipines has sickle-shaped leaves and long, thin, bright yellow flowers clustered together to form attractive balls about one-half inch in diameter. The closely related, larger native koa of the mountain forests, which is highly prized for its reddish wood, is more crooked and has similar but whitish flowers.

12. Wiliwilinui

Map: USGS Koko Head

Distance: 3 miles out and back

Time: 2.5 hours

Rating: moderate

Elevation gain: 400 feet

Footwear and special equipment: light hiking boots

Best time and season: all seasons; route along the ridge is slippery during rainfall

Distance from Waikīkī to trailhead: approx. 8 miles

Permits: free parking permit required from guard station

Highlights

The rewards of this hike include beautiful views of Koko Head, Koko Crater and the Pacific Ocean. Because the trail follows the ridge, there are numerous viewpoints on this hike. Another feature is the attractive red volcanic soil on the footpath.

Access Map

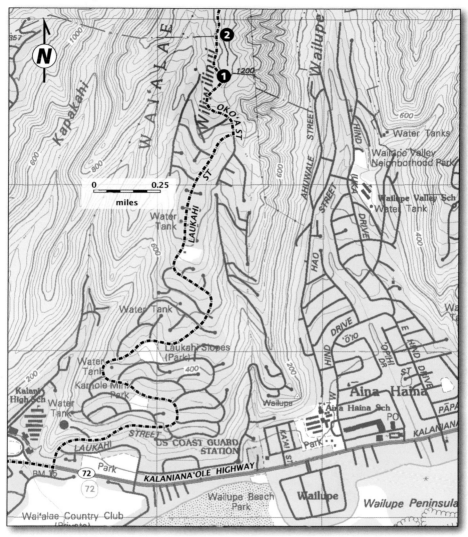

Access from Waikīkī to Trailhead

Take McCully Street *mauka* (toward the mountains) across the Ala Wai Canal and continue eight blocks, turning right (east) on South King Street. Just before reaching the Lunalilo Freeway (H-1), turn left onto Waiʻalae Avenue briefly, then take the H-1 entrance ramp on the right, merging onto the H-1 eastbound. East of exit 27, the H-1 becomes the Kalanianaʻole Highway (SR 72), and you pass the Waiʻalae Country Club Golf Course on your right. Look for Kalani High School on your left. Immediately after the school, turn left onto Laukahi Street. Stay on Laukahi Street as it winds

Trail Map

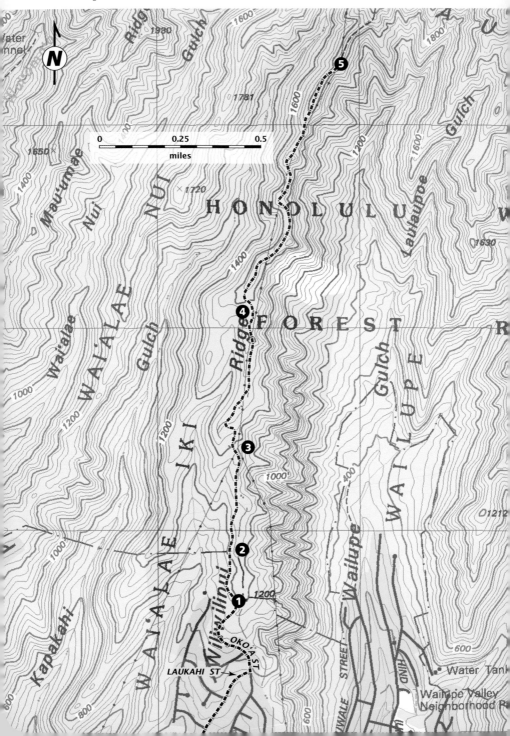

up through the Wai'alae Iki residential area.

Eventually you come to a guard station as Laukahi Street enters a gated community ahead. Ask for a hiking permit in order to proceed.

When you reach the T-intersection with Oko'a Street, go left and continue almost to the end of Oko'a. Park on the left in an area marked "Reserved for Wiliwilinui Hikers."

Trail Description

1. Pass through or around the gate at the end of Oko'a Street and begin on a paved road.

2. A water tank marks the end of the paved road.

3. Two power lines merge here.

4. Follow the wide, gently ascending dirt road that winds under the power line and ends at a vehicle turnaround. At the left of the turnaround, look for the trail, which ascends a set of steps up to the first knob on the ridge.

5. Follow the dirt trail until you meet with the power line again. This is your turnaround point. Experienced hikers may want to continue another mile to the summit. However, this part of the trail is beyond the scope of this hiking guide; it is steep and, in some areas, dangerous.

Koa Forest on Maui (pictured on p. 80)

You may be able to spot the indigenous koa tree as the road ends and the trail begins. The koa is endemic to Hawai'i and is being threatened by the invasion of non-endemic plants. It has sickle-shaped leaves and smooth, gray bark. The koa tree, which at times has a girth the size of a bus and towers over the forest, is important to Hawai'ians as building material. As alien plants are introduced, endemic trees such as the famous koa are pushed back.

13. Kuli'ou'ou Ridge

Map: USGS Koko Head

Distance: 5 miles out and back

Time: 4 hours

Rating: moderate to steep, with a narrow ridge

Elevation gain: 1800 feet

Footwear and special equipment: trail shoes; bright clothing, because this is a hunting area

Best time and season: all seasons

Distance from Waikīkī to trailhead: approx. 8 miles

Highlights

This trail is one of the easiest routes to the ridge of the Ko'olaus Range. On a clear day, the view of the windward side is stunning.

Caution: Some hikers may be nervous walking along the narrow ridge on the last stretch.

Access Map

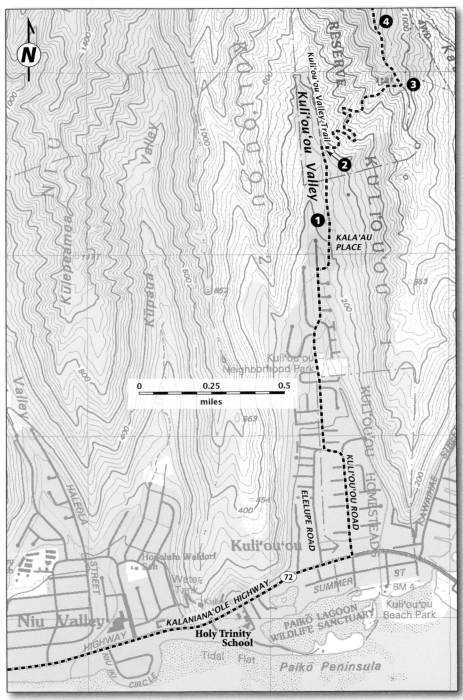

Trail Map

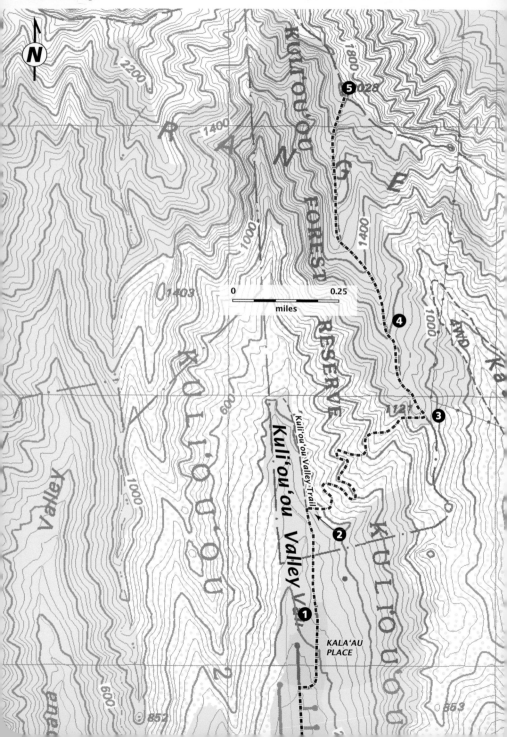

Access from Waikīkī to Trailhead

Take McCully Street *mauka* (toward the mountains) across the Ala Wai Canal and continue eight blocks, turning right (east) on South King Street. Just before reaching the Lunalilo Freeway (H-1), turn left onto Waiʻalae Avenue briefly, then take the H-1 entrance ramp on the right, merging onto the H-1 eastbound. East of exit 27, the H-1 becomes the Kalanianaʻole Highway (SR 72). At 6.5 miles from where you began the H-1, you pass the town of Aina Haina. Shortly thereafter, look for Holy Trinity School on the right. You soon pass Elelupe Road on the left. At the next intersection, turn left onto Kuliʻouʻou Road.

Stay on Kuliʻouʻou Road for 1.3 miles, passing a jog in the road, until you reach the intersection with Kalaʻau Place. Turn right onto Kalaʻau Place and park along the road. Parking is not permitted in the cul-de-sac where the trailhead is located.

Trail Description

1. Begin at the end of the cul-de-sac. A trailhead sign and a check-in station are on your right. The paved trail soon becomes a grassy road.

2. When you reach the signed intersection of the Kuli'ou'ou Valley and Kuli'ou'ou Ridge trails, make a sharp right onto the ridge trail. The Valley Trail continues straight ahead. Climb the switchbacks, avoiding spur trails.

3. After walking through a grove of ironwood trees, you reach the ridge in 45 minutes to an hour. You then pass over an eroded area and find two covered picnic tables.

4. The trail continues up a very narrow ridge with views of Koko Crater and Koko Head. There is a steep climb up plastic steps.

5. When you reach a viewpoint on the steep ridge of the Ko'olaus Range, you can see the windward side of O'ahu as well as the town of Waimanalo and Bellows Air Force Station. This viewpoint is the turnaround for this hike. (The trail that continues along the precipitous ridge to the summit is beyond the scope of this guide.) After enjoying the spectacular island scenery, retrace your steps to the trailhead.

Plants to Look For

Longleaf ironwood (gray sheoak)
A native of Australia, the longleaf ironwood tree was introduced for reforestation projects. Its slender, tufted needles resemble horsetail rushes. Because of its density, the red wood is excellent as firewood, though, as its name suggests, it is hard to cut. Nevertheless, it and common ironwood are used for a variety of woodworking and construction purposes.

14. Kuli'ou'ou Valley

Map: USGS Koko Head

Distance: 1.2 miles out and back

Time: 45 minutes

Rating: easy

Elevation gain: 300 feet

Footwear and special equipment: good walking shoes; bright clothing, because this is a hunting area

Best time and season: all seasons

Distance from Waikīkī to trailhead: approx. 8 miles

Note: Because this hike is fairly short, you may want to do hike 13, which takes you to the Kuli'ou'ou Ridge, on the same trip to make traveling to this area more worthwhile

Highlights

This short, easy trail is in a shady area with delightful pools in the rainy season.

Access from Waikīkī to Trailhead

Take McCully Street *mauka* (toward the mountains) across the Ala Wai Canal and continue eight blocks, turning right (east) on

Access Map

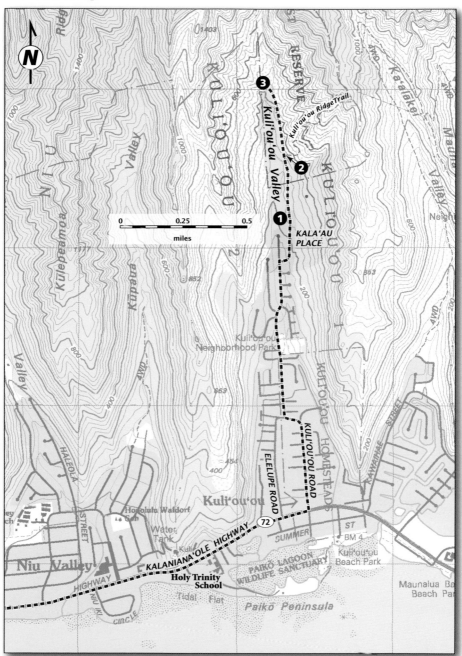

Trail Map

South King Street. Just before reaching the Lunalilo Freeway (H-1), turn left onto Wai'alae Avenue briefly, then take the H-1 entrance ramp on the right, merging onto the H-1 eastbound. East of exit 27, the H-1 becomes the Kalaniana'ole Highway (SR 72). At 6.5 miles from where you began the H-1, you pass the town of Aina Haina. Shortly thereafter, look for Holy Trinity School on the right. You soon pass Elelupe Road on the left. At the next intersection, turn left onto Kuli'ou'ou Road.

Stay on Kuli'ou'ou Road for 1.3 miles, passing a jog in the road, until you reach the intersection with Kala'au Place. Turn right onto Kala'au Place and park along the road. Parking is not permitted in the cul-de-sac where the trailhead is located.

Trail Description

1. Begin at the end of the cul-de-sac. A trailhead sign and a check-in station are on your right. The paved trail soon becomes a grassy road.

2. When you reach the signed T-junction of the Kuli'ou'ou Valley and Kuli'ou'ou Ridge trails, continue straight ahead on the valley trail. When the trail forks at a boulder garden, stay right, because the left fork crosses the boulders and is a difficult way to reach the stream.

3. Continue up a narrow trail of roots and rocks until you pass a small waterfall and pool, after which the trail becomes less distinct. Turn around when the trail becomes difficult to follow. Retrace your steps to the trailhead.

Plants to Look For

kuku'i (p. 126) and 'ulei

'Ulei

This widespread, sprawling, indigenous shrub of the rose family has small, oblong leaves arranged in pairs with clusters of white flowers. The wood was traditionally used to make digging sticks, fish spears and the *'ukeke*, a Hawai'ian musical bow instrument.

15. Koko Crater Botanical Gardens

Map: USGS Koko Head

Distance: 0.3 mile loop

Time: 1 hour

Rating: easy

Elevation gain: relatively flat

Footwear and special equipment: walking shoes and plant guide book

Best time and season: spring

Distance from Waikīkī to trailhead: approx. 13.5 miles

Fees and hours of operation: no charge; open from 9:00 AM to 4:00 PM daily, except Christmas and New Year's

Highlights

In addition to the opportunity to learn more about Hawai'ian flora, the walk inside a crater is an enjoyable aspect of the Koko Crater Botanical Gardens.

Access from Waikīkī to Trailhead

Take McCully Street *mauka* (toward the mountains)

Access Map

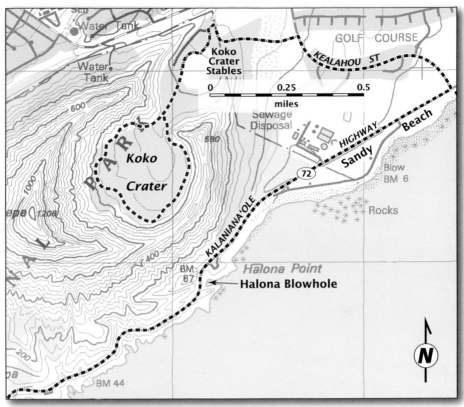

across the Ala Wai Canal and continue eight blocks, turning right (east) on South King Street. Just before reaching the Lunalilo Freeway (H-1), turn left onto Waiʻalae Avenue briefly, then take the H-1 entrance ramp on the right, merging onto the H-1 eastbound. East of exit 27, the H-1 becomes the Kalanianaʻole Highway (SR 72).

Stay on the Kalanianaʻole past Hanauma Bay. On your left, you pass the crater walls of Koko Head before reaching Halona Blowhole, which is along the shore. Stop for a look at this ocean geyser, which is especially dramatic at high tide and with turbulent seas.

After leaving Halona Blowhole, you skirt Sandy Beach Park on your right. Then turn left on Kealahou Street; the turnoff is marked by a sign for the Koko Crater Stables.

Follow the signs to the stables, continuing 0.5 miles before turning left onto an unmarked road (if you come to Hawaiʻi Kai Drive, you have gone too far). Then travel another 0.3 miles, first on a paved road and then on a dirt road, to a parking area beside the stables.

Trail Description

The Koko Botanical Gardens is to the right of the entrance to the stables.

Trail Map

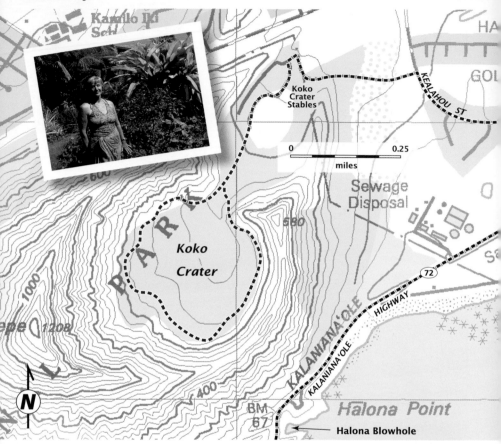

Because the area is small and visitors are encouraged to wander at will, a trail description is not needed.

Honolulu County maintains the gardens. Although there are many different plants, few are named. To make your trip to the gardens more enjoyable, bring a plant and flower guide. Two helpful pocket versions are *A Pocket Guide to Hawai'i's Flowers* by Miyano and Peebles and *A Pocket Guide to Hawai'i's Trees and Shrubs* by Douglas Pratt.

Plants to Look For

Plumeria (frangipani)

A group of tropical American natives, plumerias are now common in Hawai'i. The waxy, fragrant and long-lasting flowers, with colors ranging from white and yellow to maroon, are often used to make leis. Although the plants appear succulent, they are very drought resistant, thriving well in the desertlike ecosystem of the Koko Crater floor. When injured, plumerias exude a poisonous sap.

Plumeria (above)

Koko Crater

Koko (meaning "blood") gets its name from the red volcanic earth of the crater. Koko Crater was formed 10,000 years ago, about the same time as Diamond Head, during the most recent remnants of volcanic activity, known as the Honolulu series. The crater is in the form of a horseshoe, with a cobble cone built by eruptions from two vents. Spewed ash landed downwind, forming a summit on the southwestern side of the crater. Over time, the ash hardened into tuff, the porous-looking material that forms the walls.

At the summit of Koko Crater is the terminal of an incline railway track. During World War II, the railway provided transportation to the top of the crater. It is possible to ascend the steep outer walls of Koko Crater, but it can be dangerous, and the climb is not included in this guide.

The original name for Koko Crater was Kohelepelepe ("inner lips of the vagina"). As the legend goes, the pig demigod, Kamapua'a, desired the goddess of fire, Pele, who lived on the Big Island. Pele's sister, Kapo, detached her *kohe* ("vagina") and threw it to O'ahu to divert Kamapua'a. The trick worked—Kamapua'a followed the vagina to O'ahu and did not bother Pele further.

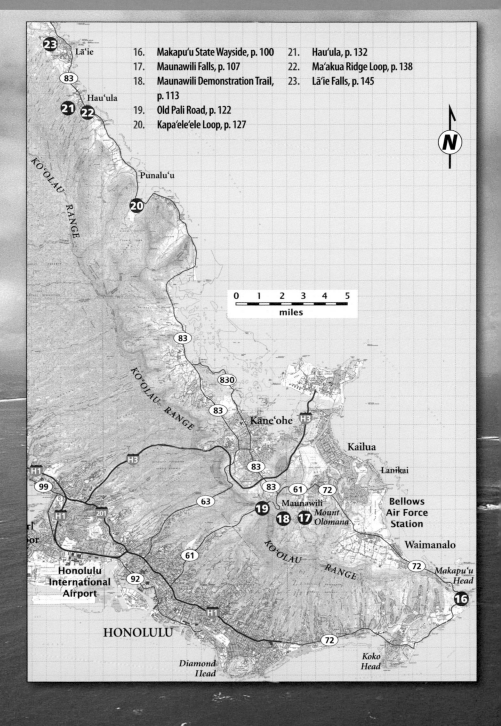

Lā'ie

Hau'ula

Punalu'u

Kāne'ohe

Kailua

Lanikai

Bellows
Air Force
Station

Waimanalo

Maunawili

Mount
Olomana

Makapu'u
Head

Honolulu
International
Airport

HONOLULU

Diamond
Head

Koko
Head

KO'OLAU RANGE

0 1 2 3 4 5
miles

N

16. Makapuʻu State Wayside

Map: USGS Koko Head

Distance: 2 miles out and back

Time: 1.5 hours

Rating: easy

Elevation gain: 520 feet

Footwear and special equipment: walking shoes, sun hat and light wind jacket

Best time and season: October to May for possible whale sightings

Distance from Waikīkī to trailhead: approx. 13 miles

Highlights

Makapuʻu ("bulging eye") Head is the most easterly point of Oʻahu and offers a spectacular view of windward Oʻahu. The route skirts along steep cliffs, with views of the ocean and, in the distance, the faint outline of the Island of Molokai. From the lookout at the top, there are views of a lighthouse perched on the cliffs

Access Map

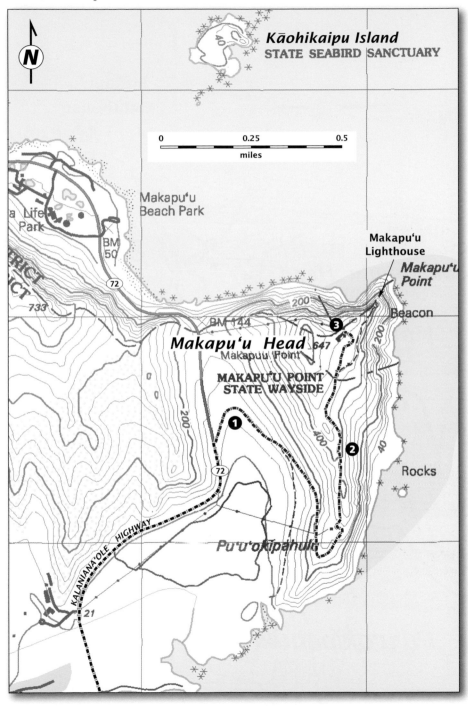

Kāohikaipu Island
STATE SEABIRD SANCTUARY

0   0.25   0.5
miles

Makapu'u
Beach Park

Makapu'u
Lighthouse

Makapu'u
Point

Beacon

Makapu'u Head
Makapuu Point

MAKAPU'U POINT
STATE WAYSIDE

Rocks

KALANIANA'OLE HIGHWAY

Pu'u'o Kipahulu

Trail Map

Makapuʻu
Lighthouse

Makapuʻu Point

Beacon

Makapuʻu Point

Makapuʻu Head 647

Makapuu Point

MAKAPUʻU POINT
STATE WAYSIDE

Rocks

Puʻuʻokipahulu

BM 144

200

200

400

40

0   0.25
miles

N

72

below Makapuʻu and of dazzling Waimanalo Bay, one of Oʻahu's most challenging surfing areas.

Access from Waikīkī to Trailhead

Take McCully Street *mauka* (toward the mountains) across the Ala Wai Canal and continue eight blocks, turning right (east) on South King Street. Just before reaching the Lunalilo Freeway (H-1), turn left onto Waiʻalae Avenue briefly, then take the H-1 entrance ramp on the right, merging onto the H-1 eastbound. East of exit 27, the H-1 becomes the Kalanianaʻole Highway (SR 72). Stay on the highway past Hanauma Bay, the town of Hawaiʻi Kai and Sandy Beach. Just after the highway turns inland and begins to rise to a pass, look for a paved road to the right, 3.8 miles from Hanauma Bay. Park on the side of the highway or continue a further 0.5 miles to a small parking area on the right and walk back to the trailhead.

Trail Description

1. The route is on a narrow, paved road that previously provided vehicle access to Makapuʻu Head. There are two gates, both easy to get

View from Makapu'u Trail with Koko Head in the distance and Bishop Estate land below

around, one at the trailhead and a second gate as the road begins to climb. The road winds up Makapu'u through a dry area vegetated with koa haole and kiawe. The delightful ocean bay below the trail is located on land held by the Bishop Estate (see p. 158).

2. To the right as you ascend is a rock formation locally known as Pele's Chair. As the road climbs, look to the southwest for views of Koko Crater and Koko Head.

3. Below the lookout at the top of the point is the well-known Makapu'u Point Lighthouse. To the north are two island bird sanctuaries: Manana and Kāohikaipu. Between October and May, you may be able to spot humpback whales offshore.

Humpback Whales

Listed as endangered by CITES, humpback whales have been recovering, now with a worldwide population of 10,000. The whales migrate south from the Alaskan waters of the North Pacific to congregate in Hawai'ian waters to mate, birth and nurse their young. These cetaceans may reach up to 45 feet in length, occasionally longer. The front flippers are very long, almost one-third of the length of the whale. Humpbacks frequently jump completely out of the water (breaching). When a whale dives deeply (sounds), you may see its large, scalloped flukes come up off the water's surface. Humpbacks are renowned for their complex and lengthy "songs."

Makapu'u Point Lighthouse (above)

Mānana Island (also known as Rabbit Island)

Shaped like the head of a rabbit, this island was once inhabited by feral rabbits. Now closed to the public, it is a breeding sanctuary for seabirds, including the sooty tern, wedge-tailed shearwater, brown noddy, Bulwer's petrel and red-tailed tropicbird.

Manana Island (above), lookout (below)

Kāohikaipu Island (also known as Turtle Island and Black Rock)

Restricted to the public, this island is a breeding sanctuary for seabirds, including the wedge-tailed shearwater, Bulwer's petrel and black noddy.

Bunkers Built by James Jones

Near the top of Makapu'u Point are "pillboxes" carved into the hillside in 1941 by James Jones and Company F, 27th Regiment, 25th Division, to defend the island. Jones later went on to write a number of books based on his experiences. *From Here to Eternity* and *A Thin Red Line* were made into popular films; he wrote about the Makapu'u pillboxes in *Pistol*.

Moloka'i, Maui and Lana'i

Moloka'i is usually visible from Makupu'u, and, on a clear day, Maui and Lana'i can also be seen. Moloka'i is about 30 miles across the Kaiwi Channel. Regular paddling races across the channel take place each May (Kaiwi Challenge Relay, in one-person canoes; Kanaka Ikaika Kayak Race, in solo kayaks and canoes), July (the Moloka'i to O'ahu Paddleboard Race), September (Na Wahine O Ke Kai, in women's outrigger canoes) and October (Moloka'i Hoe, in men's outrigger canoes).

17. Maunawili Falls

Highlights

This hike features cascading Maunawili ("twisted mountain") Falls and the deep pool at its base. As well, be sure to take in the sweeping views from the ridge above the stream.

Access from Waikīkī to Trailhead

Take McCully Street *mauka* (toward the mountains) across the Lunalilo Freeway (H-1) and immediately go left onto Dole Street, which you stay on for one block.

Map: USGS Koko Head and Honolulu

Distance: 2.5 miles out and back

Time: 2.5 hours

Rating: moderate, with several stream crossings

Elevation gain: 400 feet

Footwear and special equipment: light hiking boots; optional river shoes and hiking stick to help navigate the several stream crossings more safely

Best time and season: all seasons; avoid during heavy rainstorms

Distance from Waikīkī to trailhead: approx. 11 miles

Caution: if you have no open sores, it is probably safer to wade across rather than jump from rock to rock; however, stream crossings can be hazardous, especially during or immediately following heavy rainfall

Special considerations: pets are not allowed on this trail

Photo: Maunawili Stream—cross with caution, especially in high water.

Access Map

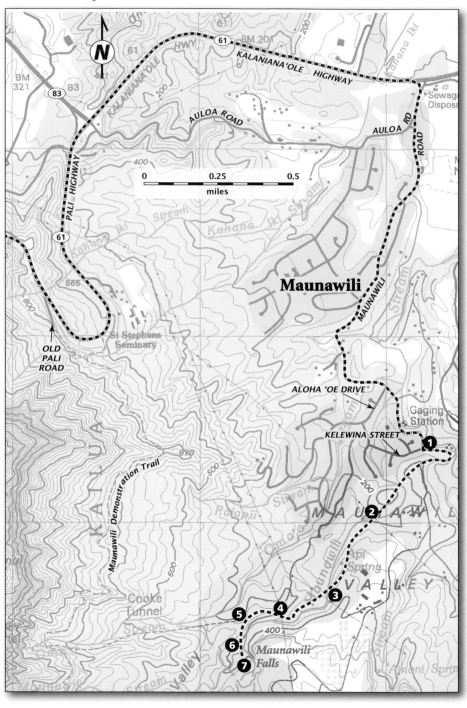

Turn left onto Alexander Street and, where it ends, go right onto the H-1 on-ramp to merge onto the H-1 westbound.

At exit 21B, turn onto the Pali Highway (SR 61) and stay on it as it passes Nuʻuanu Pali State Wayside and descends to the windward side of Oʻahu. Pass Auloa Road at a four-way intersection —Kamehameha Highway (SR 83) is to the left— and continue straight ahead, now on the Kalanianaʻole Highway (SR 61). Turn right at the second intersection with Auloa. You've now traveled 9 miles on the Pali and Kalanianaʻole highways. Where the exit forks, keep right.

The streets in the Maunawili subdivision are poorly marked, so a good road map can help locate the trailhead.

Continue an additional 0.1 miles to a narrow fork and veer left onto Maunawili Road. Stay on Maunawili Road as it winds through the subdivision. Look for parking near Aloha ʻOe Drive and walk about 0.3 miles

Trail Map

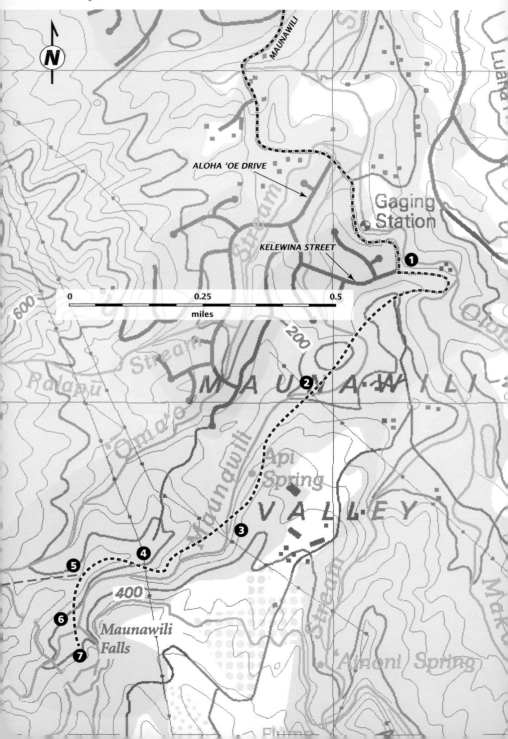

to the trailhead, which is marked by a gate to the left where Maunawili Road ends at Kelewina Street. There is no parking at the actual trailhead.

Trail Description

1. Pass around the gate and begin the hike on a paved road. Walk a few hundred feet and look for the marked trail to the right. Several informational signs here explain the archeological significance of the area. The trail is well maintained in the first section. After descending a set of stairs, you briefly parallel the stream before making the first of several stream crossings. On the other side, take the trail that leads up over boulders and into the forest. (The new trail that has recently opened up along the stream also leads to the falls.)

2. Cross the stream a second time; you are now walking through heavy tropical vegetation.

3. Cross the stream a third time and ascend a hillside with the stream below; again, new trails have recently opened up closer to the river.

4. Climb the two sets of steps to an open area with an excellent view of the Ko'olau Range. Stay left on the main trial where a spur on the right leads to a viewpoint.

5. When you reach a junction with a trail connecting to the Maunawili Demonstration Trail (see hike 18), stay left and descend the steep steps to the river.

6. Depending on the height of the water, you may have to cross the creek two more times before you reach the base of the falls. In low water, you will cross a small stream entering Maunawili before walking along the stream edge to a pool and the waterfall.

7. You soon reach the waterfall and pool. On warm weekends, the pool is a favorite spot for daring youth, who jump from the cliffs into the water. Retrace your steps to the trailhead.

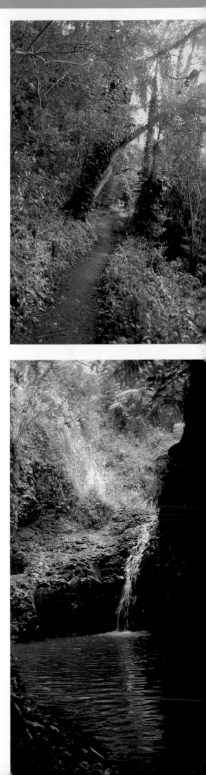

Plants to Look For

Guava

Introduced in the 1800s by a Spanish immigrant, the guava is now a staple in Hawai'ian fruit drinks. The fruit, though tart, is edible when picked ripe from the trees. The guava tree is small and, when not bearing its large, yellowish fruit, can be identified by its brushlike, white flowers and by its smooth, reddish brown bark marked by irregular green patches. The related strawberry guava, with an edible fruit resembling cherries, has become invasive in Hawai'i.

Guava (above)

18. Maunawili Demonstration Trail

Highlights

This fairly new trail offers wonderful views of the windward side of O'ahu and the spectacular mountain ridges. After a rainfall, many small waterfalls can be seen cascading above and below the trail, along with delightful tropical pools. When you reach the town of Waimanalo, stay a while to enjoy one of the local

Map: USGS Honolulu and Koko Head

Distance: 8 miles one way (10.5 miles if you start at the Pali Lookout and walk out to the bus stop in Waimanalo)

Time: 5 hours

Rating: moderate

Elevation change: 650-foot descent

Footwear and special equipment: trail shoes; optional cell phone to

arrange pickup at the Waimanalo trailhead

Best time and season: best after a rainfall to see waterfalls

Distance from Waikīkī to trailhead: approx. 10 miles

Caution: heavy rains may cause flooding of creeks and rockfalls

Note: arrange for transportation at the Waimanalo trailhead at the end of the hike

Photo: Mt. Olomana (Forked Hill)

Access Map

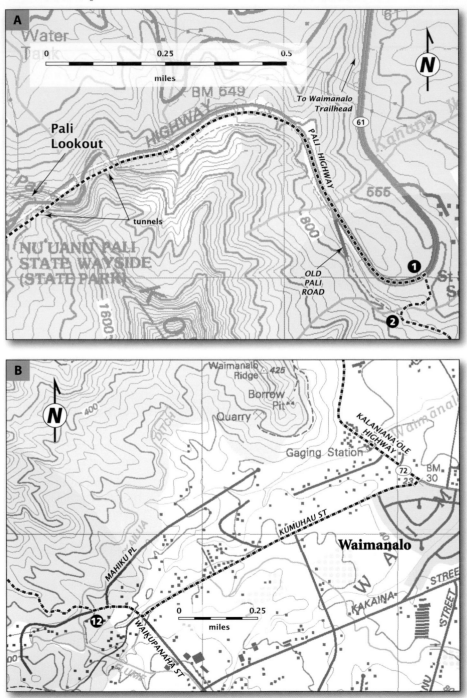

eateries and meet the generous, friendly residents.

Access from Waikīkī to the Pali Road Trailhead (Map A)

Take McCully Street *mauka* (toward the mountains) across the Lunalilo Freeway (H-1) and immediately go left onto Dole Street, which you stay on for one block. Turn left onto Alexander Street and, where it ends, go right onto the H-1 on-ramp to merge onto the H-1 westbound.

At exit 21B, turn onto the Pali Highway (SR 61). At 5.4 miles from the beginning of the Pali Highway (*see Map A*), you pass Nu'uanu Pali State Park and begin to descend to the windward side of O'ahu. Soon afterward, you reach a hairpin turn; the trailhead is located here on the right. Signs prohibit parking, but some people do so anyway. We recommend that you arrange to be dropped off at the hairpin turn and picked up at the Waimanalo trailhead at the end.

Trailhead at the viewpoint on the Pali Highway

Mt. Olomana

Alternatively, leave a vehicle in the nearby commercial area (about 1.5 miles from the trail end). It is about a 15-minute drive between the two trailheads. You can also park at the Pali Lookout or take a bus there and walk the additional mile to the trailhead.

Access from the Pali Lookout to the Waimanalo Trailhead (Map B)

Continue along the Pali Highway (*see Map A*). After the intersection with

Auloa Road and the Kamehameha Highway (SR 83), you are on the Kalaniana'ole Highway (SR 61). When the Castle Medical Center appears on the left, keep right to stay on the Kalaniana'ole Highway (SR 72); going straight would put you on Kailua Road (SR 61).

Continue south on the Kalaniana'ole Highway, passing the Olomana Golf Links on your left. Pass Flamingo Street on the right and take the next right, Kumuhau Street (*see Map B*). Continue to the T-intersection with Waikupanaha Street and go right; continue until you pass Mahiku Place. Soon you will see the sign for the trailhead on your right.

If you are picking up hikers, they will appear here. If you are leaving a vehicle, do not park here, because vehicles have been vandalized at this remote site. Instead, park in the commercial area of town and walk from the trailhead. You can also take a bus from downtown Waimanalo or call a taxi to meet you at the trailhead.

Trail Map

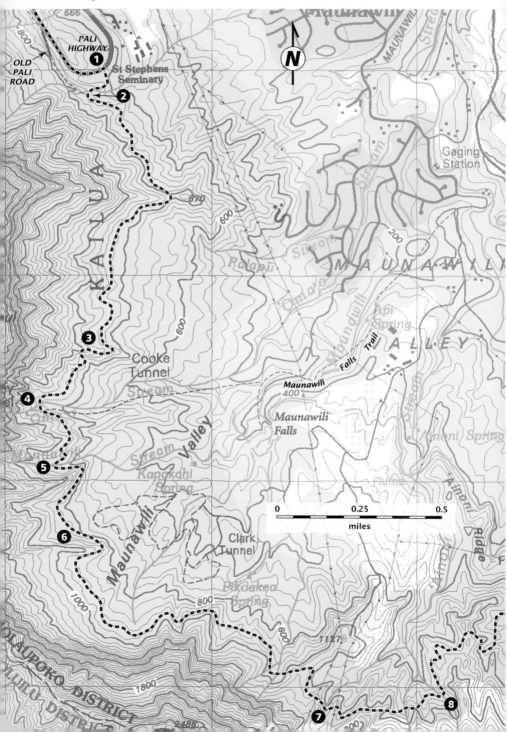

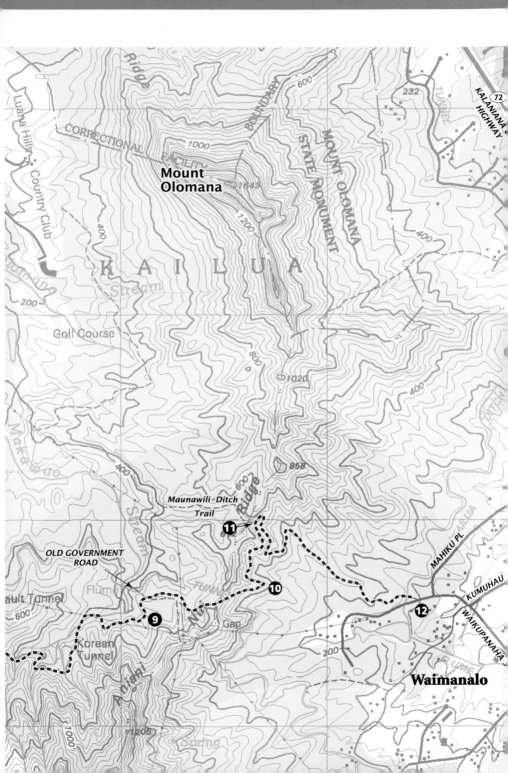

Trail Description

From the viewpoint on the hairpin turn on the Pali Highway, you can see the signed trail leading into the forest and toward the mountains. Note that the markers along the trail indicating mileage may not be correct. One marker indicates 6.3 miles to the end, whereas, using GPS and a pedometer, we estimated the distance to be closer to 5 miles.

1.   Before leaving the viewpoint, look to the east to see spectacular Mount Olomana ("forked hill"). The trail crosses a creekbed and leads up a set of steps.

2.   Keep left where the trail intersects a path on your right that climbs to the Old Pali Road; you soon pass a water tank. There are steep sections leading up and down from where you cross the creekbeds.

3.   As you cross over a spur ridge, the trail makes a sharp right turn.

4.   Continue along the well-defined trail until you reach a signed intersection, where you go straight (the left fork leads down to Maunawili Falls). The trail curves around the slopes of the Koʻolau Range from ravine to ravine, often with excellent views of windward Oʻahu.

5.   From a viewpoint, you can see fields and farm buildings in the valley below.

6.   When you reach a trail marker that indicates 6.3 miles to the end of the trail, you can see the steep slopes of the mountains above you, and you have views of Kailua in the distance.

7.   Just past trail marker mile 5, you cross under a set of power lines and round a ridge with power poles at the top.

8.   Pass several weeping walls, which become waterfalls in rainy weather. Look for a pool below the trail at the second weeping wall; here the water streams over a steep, black rock face. The extreme steepness of the eastern side of the Koʻolau Range resulted when the eastern flank of the Koʻolau volcano collapsed about two million years ago.

9.   After a sign that says "No Horses," you cross under a second power line and continue straight through the clearing. On the far side, take the trail marked with the Na Ala Hele sign; the left branch, marked "No Trespassing," is the Old Government Road. The trail skirts below the Aniani Nui Ridge. Crest the ridge to a viewpoint of Kailua, Waimanalo and the ocean.

10. After the signs "No Horses Beyond This Point" and "Maunawili Demonstration Trail," continue straight downhill at the next junction; the left branch is gated.

11. You soon reach the signed Maunawili Ditch Trail on your left. Continue straight, taking the wide path to your right.

12. When you reach the Waimanalo trailhead, either have a friend or taxi pick you up or walk out, about 1.5 miles, to the commercial area where you parked earlier or where you can catch a bus.

19. Old Pali Road

Map: USGS Honolulu

Distance: 2 miles out and back

Time: 1 hour

Rating: easy

Elevation gain: 350 feet

Footwear and special equipment: walking shoes

Best time and season: all seasons

Distance from Waikīkī to trailhead: approx. 9 miles

Highlights

The panoramic views of windward O'ahu are spectacular, as are the awesome views of the Ko'olau Range. The trailhead has historic significance: it was on these windward cliffs in 1795 that Kamehameha defeated the O'ahu forces in the final battle for the control of the island.

Access Map

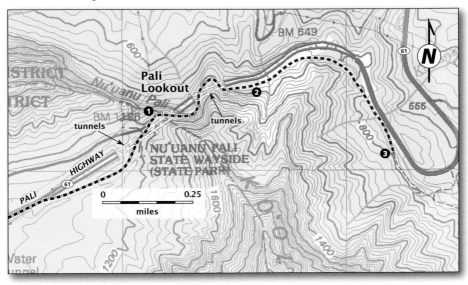

Access from Waikīkī to Trailhead

Take McCully Street *mauka* (toward the mountains) across the Lunalilo Freeway (H-1) and immediately go left onto Dole Street, which you stay on for one block. Turn left onto Alexander Street and, where it ends, go right onto the H-1 on-ramp to merge onto the H-1 westbound.

At exit 21B, turn onto the Pali Highway (SR 61). At 5.4 miles from the entrance to the Pali Highway, you reach Nu'uanu Pali State Wayside. Park here, on the right.

Nu'uana Pali

Trail Map

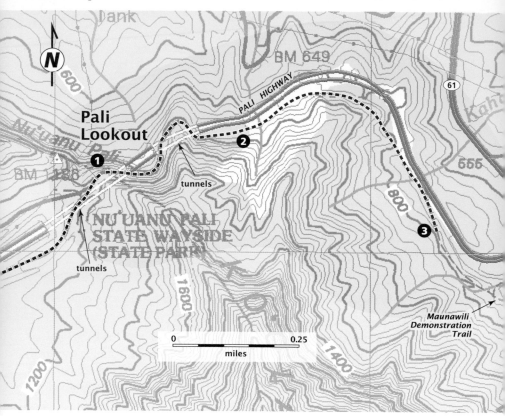

Trail Description

1. From the parking lot, walk to the lookout, where two trails lead to the Old Pali Road (or Highway). Take either trail, because they converge after a short distance. Once you are on the old road, walk through or around the gate and proceed down the Old Pali Road. Built in 1932 and replaced by the current highway about 30 years later, the roadbed is becoming overgrown as plants reclaim it.

2. Steep cliffs rise up on your right, and the sweeping landscape of the windward side of Oʻahu drops away on the left. As you proceed down the old highway,

you can see the towns and bays of Kailua and Kāneʻohe.

3. Continue on the old road until you reach a high wire fence where the trail narrows. This is your turnaround point. (The trail that continues through the vegetation connects to the Maunawili Demonstration Trail.)

Kamehameha the Great, 1758–1819

Kamehameha ("the lonely one") was a skilled warrior and leader from the Big Island. He became known as the ruler who, through a series of bloody battles, united the Hawaiʻian Islands under one monarchy. In 1790, he vanquished his foes on Maui with the assistance of cannons taken from the *Fair American*, a ship captured by the Hawaiʻians. Oʻahu was next. In 1795, a decisive battle took place along the Nuʻuanu Pali. He tried twice to conquer Kauaʻi, but storms repelled his army. Kamehameha invited chief Kaʻumuʻaliʻi, of Kauaʻi, to Oʻahu and, through rewards and threats, forced the chief to cede Kauaʻi, thus uniting the islands in 1810. A bronze statue of King Kamehameha stands in Honolulu on South King between Mililani and Punchbowl Streets. King Kamehameha Day is a state holiday celebrated on June 11.

Kukuʻi (above)

Plants to Look For

koa haole (p. 26), kukuʻi and
pau o Hiʻiaka (p. 204)

Kukuʻi (candlenut)

The state tree of Hawaiʻi, kukuʻi was likely brought to the islands by the first Hawaiʻians, and it figures in a number of native legends. A medium-sized tree, it prefers moist valleys. Kukuʻi flowers are white, and the foliage is a distinctive pale green. As with maples, the leaves have several distinct lobes. The oil-rich nuts were traditionally used for lighting, with each nut lasting about 15 minutes, and for the most prestigious leis. The nuts are an ingredient in foods such as poke, and the oil is commercially used in skin creams and shampoos. The Hawaiʻian people tradition-ally used kukuʻi wood to make gunwales and seats for outrigger canoes.

20. Kapa'ele'ele Loop

Highlights

This trail features two Hawai'ian shrines relating to the fish harvest in Kahana Bay. As well, interpretative signs help newcomers to O'ahu become acquainted with the beautiful variety of plant life. Finally, the views of Kahana Bay from this short trail are excellent.

Map: USGS Kahana

Distance: 1 mile loop

Time: 30 minutes

Rating: easy

Elevation gain: 100 feet

Footwear and special equipment: walking shoes

Best time and season: all seasons

Distance from Waikīkī to trailhead: approx. 30 miles

Access Map

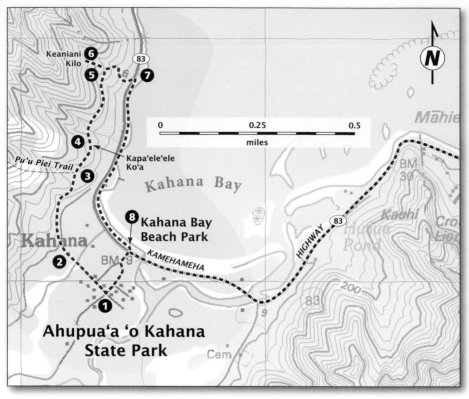

Access from Waikīkī to Trailhead

Take McCully Street *mauka* (toward the mountains) across the Lunalilo Freeway (H-1) and immediately go left onto Dole Street, which you stay on for one block. Turn left onto Alexander Street and, where it ends, go right onto the H-1 on-ramp to merge onto the H-1 westbound.

Continue on the H-1 for 3.6 miles and take the Likelike Highway (SR 63) at exit 20A.

From the entrance onto Likelike Highway, continue 7.3 miles and exit onto the Kehekili Highway (SR 83), which eventually merges with the Kamehameha Highway (still SR 83). Pass the oceanside Kualoa Regional Park and look out over the bay to see Mokoliʻi Island (also known as Chinaman's Hat).

Continue north, soon passing the ruins of an old sugar mill on your left.

After you pass the Crouching Lion Restaurant, the highway circles the edge of Kahana Bay. Turn left into Ahupuaʻa ʻo Kahana State Park.

Drive a short distance and park at the orientation center (the green building on the right).

The trailhead is to the right of the orientation center.

Trail Description

1. Your route begins on a gravel road. Pass a number of private dwellings and continue onto a dirt road. The route passes under a power line; then, at a signed junction, goes left onto a trail into the forest.

2. Interpretative signs along this part of the trail identify the plants and their uses.

3. Pass a dry creekbed, where there is a T-junction with the Pu'u Piei Trail. The left fork is the Pu'u Piei Trail, which climbs up a steep ridge to the summit of Pu'u Piei. Stay right on the Kapa'ele'ele Trail.

4. The trail ascends to the ancient fish shrine Kapa'ele'ele Ko'a.

Trail Map

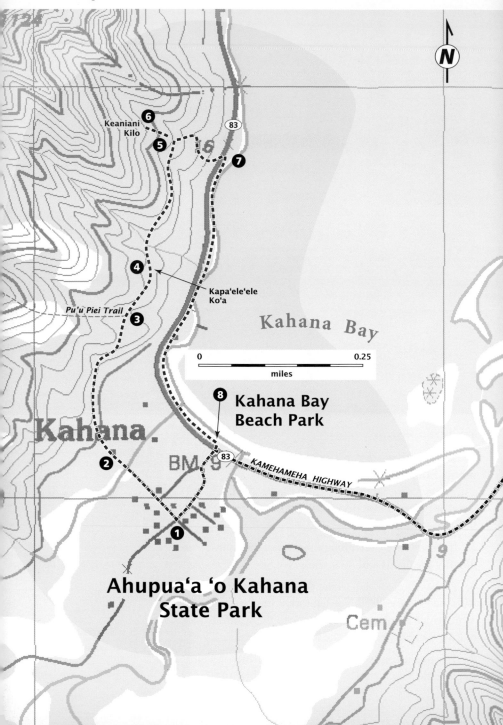

Keaniani Kilo

Kapaʻeleʻele Koʻa

Puʻu Piei Trail

Kahana Bay

0   0.25
miles

Kahana Bay
Beach Park

Kahana

BM 9

KAMEHAMEHA HIGHWAY

**Ahupuaʻa ʻo Kahana
State Park**

Cem

5. When you arrive at another T-junction, take the left trail and go a short distance to Keaniani Kilo. This lookout, now considered a shrine, was used by Hawaiʻians to alert fishers when a school of fish entered the bay.

6. Retrace your steps to the Kapaʻeleʻele Trail, where you take a left turn and head down to the bay.

7. Cross the highway to Kahana Bay Beach Park and walk along the beach.

8. Again, cross the highway at the entrance to Ahupuaʻa ʻo Kahana State Park. Walk back to the parking area at the orientation center.

Why are the Kahana Valley Trails not included? As this book goes to press, the many spur trails created by hunters in the Kahana Valley make it difficult to remain on official trails. If and when the trail marking is improved, we hope to include them in future editions of this guide.

21. Hauʻula

Map: USGS Hauʻula

Distance: 2.5 mile loop

Time: 2 hours

Rating: easy, but with two stream crossings on rocks

Elevation gain: 700 feet

Footwear and special equipment: trail shoes; bright clothing, because the area is open to hunting

Best time and season: all seasons

Distance from Waikīkī to trailhead: approx. 33 miles

Caution: the stream crossings can be slippery during or after heavy rain

Note: As of this writing, the Maʻakua Gulch Trail is closed because of the danger of flash floods and is not likely to reopen unless Sacred Falls State Park is reopened as well (see hike 22)

Pictured here: Cook pine forest on the Hauʻula Trail

Highlights

This hike is an easy stroll through a beautiful iron-wood forest; part of the enjoyment is visiting the delightful town of Hauʻula. It is possible to hike both the Hauʻula Trail and the Maʻakua Ridge Loop (see hike 22) in one day, giving you a most pleasant outing.

Access from Waikīkī to Trailhead

Take McCully Street *mauka* (toward the mountains) across the Lunalilo Freeway

Access Map

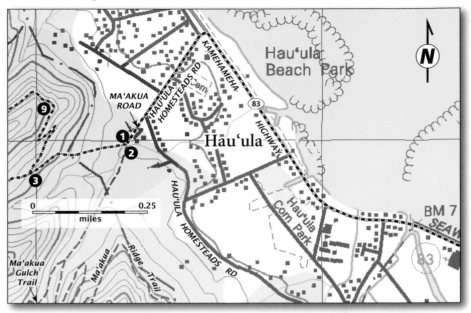

(H-1) and immediately go left onto Dole Street, which you stay on for one block. Turn left onto Alexander Street and, where it ends, go right onto the H-1 on-ramp to merge onto the H-1 westbound.

Continue on the H-1 for 3.6 miles and take the Likelike Highway (SR 63) at exit 20A.

From the entrance onto the Likelike Highway, continue 7.3 miles and exit onto the Kehekili Highway (SR 83),

Trail Map

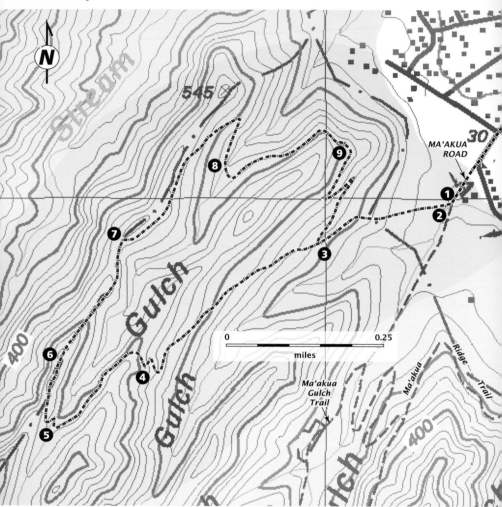

which eventually merges with the Kamehameha Highway (still SR 83). Pass the oceanside Kualoa Regional Park and look out over the bay to see Mokoliʻi Island (also known as Chinaman's Hat).

Continue north, soon passing the ruins of an old sugar mill on your left. Pass Kahana Bay and the village of Punaluʻu.

From Punaluʻu, continue a further 3.3 miles to the town of Hauʻula. Turn left onto Hauʻula Homestead Road (the second time you see this road, across from Hauʻula Beach Park); a church marks this turnoff.

Stay on Hauʻula Homestead Road for about 0.2 miles; where it veers left, continue straight onto Maʻakua Road and drive to the end. To avoid possible vandalism here, you may prefer to park back at the Hauʻula Beach Park or elsewhere in town and walk the 0.5 miles (or less) to the trailhead.

Trail Description

1. At the end of Maʻakua Road, pass around a chain on a paved road and look for a check-in station and trail signs. The sign shows three trails: Maʻakua, Hauʻula and Maʻakua Gulch (closed in 2002 because of the danger of flash floods).

2. Hike up the road and find the Hauʻula trailhead sign on your right. Take a sharp right to begin the Hauʻula Trail (marked at this writing) and shortly cross a streambed.

3. After gentle switchbacks, you reach a fork (unmarked at this writing) where you turn left. The trail on your right will be your return route.

4. When you reach a spur trail in an open area, stay right on the main trail as you descend.

5. Cross over the stream that runs across rocks above a pool. This crossing can be hazardous during heavy rainstorms. You soon have a view over the Kaipapa'u Valley to the northwest. Avoid a spur trail near here, keeping right to stay on the main trail.

6. You pass another viewpoint before descending steps.

7. Cross an eroded area with the distinctive red volcanic soil exposed.

8. Use caution at the second creek crossing, where the stream trickles over rocks.

9. Round a ridge, where there is a view of Hau'ula and the ocean, and close the loop, turning left to retrace your steps back to the trailhead; if you still have enough energy and daylight, consider also doing the Ma'akua Ridge Loop (see hike 22).

Plants To Look For

Cook pine (p. 57), ironwood (p. 89), octopus plant and strawberry guava (p. 112)

Octopus plant (umbrella tree, schefflera)

A fast-growing, invasive evergreen, this stand-alone small tree or climber blooms in sprays of long, red "octopus arms." Common as a houseplant, it rarely flowers indoors. The dark green leaves grow in umbrella-shaped rosettes of six to ten. It favors wet lowlands. A number of these trees are easy to spot from the Hau'ula and Ma'akua Trails.

Photo, right: Octopus plant

22. Ma'akua Ridge Loop

Map: USGS Hau'ula

Distance: 2.5 miles, out and back plus loop

Time: 2.5 hours

Rating: easy

Elevation gain: 800 feet

Footwear and special equipment: trail shoes; bright clothing, because the area is open to hunting

Best time and season: all seasons

Distance from Waikīkī to trailhead: approx. 33 miles

Note: As of this writing, the Ma'akua Gulch Trail is closed because of the danger of flash floods and is not likely to reopen unless Sacred Falls State Park is reopened as well

Highlights

This hike includes an especially interesting geological feature—a narrow saddle along a lava ridge. It is possible to hike both the Ma'akua Ridge Loop and the Hau'ula Trail (see hike 21) in one day, giving you a most pleasant outing.

Access Map

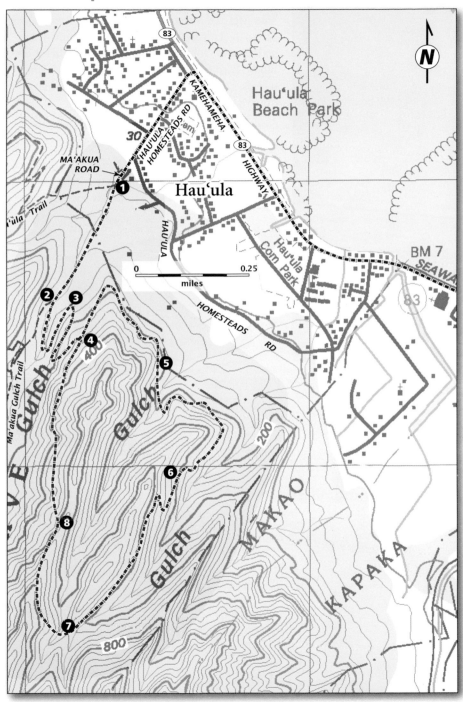

Access from Waikīkī to Trailhead

Take McCully Street *mauka* (toward the mountains) across the Lunalilo Freeway (H-1) and immediately go left onto Dole Street, which you stay on for one block. Turn left onto Alexander Street and, where it ends, go right onto the H-1 on-ramp to merge onto the H-1 westbound.

Continue on the H-1 for 3.6 miles and take the Likelike Highway (SR 63) at exit 20A.

From the entrance onto the Likelike Highway, continue 7.3 miles and exit onto the Kehekili Highway (SR 83), which eventually merges with

Narrow saddle on Maakua Ridge Trail (above)

the Kamehameha Highway (still SR 83). Pass the oceanside Kualoa Regional Park and look out over the bay to see Mokoli'i Island (also known as Chinaman's Hat).

Continue north, soon passing the ruins of an old sugar mill on your left. Pass Kahana Bay and the village of Punalu'u.

From Punalu'u, continue a further 3.3 miles to the town of Hau'ula. Turn left onto Hau'ula Homestead Road (the second time you see this road, across from Hau'ula Beach Park); a church marks this turnoff.

Stay on Hau'ula Homestead Road for about 0.2 miles; where it veers left, continue straight onto Ma'akua Road and drive to the end. To avoid possible vandalism here, you may prefer to park back at the Hau'ula Beach Park or elsewhere in town and walk the 0.5 miles (or less) to the trailhead.

Ironwood forest (above)

Trail Description

1. At the end of Ma'akua Road, pass around a chain on a paved road and look for a check-in station and trail signs. The sign shows three trails: Ma'akua, Hau'ula and Ma'akua Gulch (closed in 2002 because of the danger of flash floods). Begin the hike up the road and pass the Hau'ula trailhead sign on your right.

2. Continue about 300 feet farther along the paved road to the Ma'akua Ridge trailhead on your left. The trail sign identifies the trail as the Papali/Ma'akua Ridge Trail. Take this trail, and almost immediately you cross a streambed. Ascend on switchbacks to soon reach a viewpoint where the ocean is visible.

3. A picnic shelter is located on a spur off the trail to the left.

4. A bench marks the beginning of the loop portion of this hike. Although you can hike the loop in either direction, we describe a clockwise

Trail Map

route that begins to your left; the trail to the right will be your return route.

5. You soon reach a black rock outcrop and then cross a streambed.

6. The trail crosses a narrow saddle along a ridge—one of the most fascinating landforms on our many O'ahu hikes.

7. Cross another creekbed.

8. The trail reaches the top of the ridge and then drops down to close the loop. Take the left fork at the bench and retrace your steps to the trailhead; if you still have enough energy and daylight, consider also doing the Hau'ula Trail (see hike 21).

Sacred Falls State Park

In 1999, an immense rockfall into the gorge at the base of Kaliuwa'a Falls (Sacred Falls), about 2 miles due south of Hau'ula, killed eight people and injured 34. Following this tragedy and subsequent litigation (a number of accidents caused by rockfalls and flash floods had occurred previously in the park), both Sacred Falls and the nearby Ma'akua Gulch Trail, which poses similar dangers, were closed.

Hala tree (above), swamp mahogany (center)

Plants to Look For

Christmas berry (p. 190), swamp mahogany, octopus plant (p. 137) and hala tree

Hala tree (pandanus, screwpine)

Sometimes called screwpine because of its long, narrow leaves (*lau*) with sawtoothed edges arranged in a spiral, this tree is believed to be indigenous to Hawai'i. It prefers moist areas and is distinguished by the numerous prop roots around the base of the trunk and the pineapple-like fruit that it bears. The plant is a traditional source of fiber, food and medicines.

Swamp mahogany

Introduced from Australia for reforestation about 100 years ago, swamp mahogany is the most common of a fair number of eucalyptus species found on O'ahu. Eucalyptus trees typically have long, narrow leaves, brushy, white flowers and a distinctive camphor aroma. The swamp mahogany grows to 100 feet tall and is distinguished by its deeply furrowed bark.

23. Lā'ie Falls

Highlights

This trail passes through varied landscapes with a range of vegetation types and features two beautiful, remote waterfalls.

Access from Waikīkī to Trailhead

Take McCully Street *mauka* (toward the mountains) across the Lunalilo Freeway (H-1) and immediately go left onto Dole Street, which you stay on for one block. Turn left onto Alexander Street and, where it ends, go right onto the H-1 on-ramp to merge onto the H-1 westbound.

Map: USGS Kahuku

Distance: 7 miles out and back

Time: 4 hours

Rating: moderate to difficult; the first section of the hike is eroded and difficult in rainy weather; the descent to the falls is steep

Elevation gain: 600 feet

Footwear and special equipment: light hiking boots

Best time and season: closed on Sundays; all seasons; use extreme caution or avoid the hike down to the falls during or just after heavy rainfalls because of the risk of flash floods

Distance from Waikīkī to trailhead: approx. 36 miles

Permits: obtain a permit from Hawai'i Reserves Inc., at 55–510 Kamehameha Highway, Lā'ie; phone: (808) 293-9201; open 9:00 AM to 4:30 PM, Monday to Friday; ask for a permit to be faxed to you if you plan to hike on a Saturday

Caution: during or after heavy rain, there is a danger of flash floods at the falls

Access Map

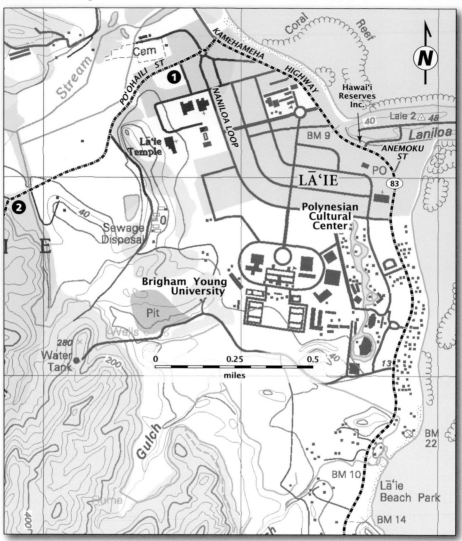

Continue on the H-1 for 3.6 miles and take the Likelike Highway (SR 63) at exit 20A.

From the entrance onto the Likelike Highway, continue 7.3 miles and exit onto the Kehekili Highway (SR 83), which eventually merges with the Kamehameha Highway (still SR 83).

Pass the oceanside Kualoa Regional Park and look out over the bay to see Mokoli'i Island (also known as Chinaman's Hat).

Continue north, soon passing the ruins of an old sugar mill on your left. Pass Kahana Bay, the village of Punalu'u and the town of Hau'ula.

After you pass the Polynesian Cultural Center, continue a short distance to the town of Lā'ie. Pick up your permit at the Lā'ie Shopping Center, then continue on past Lā'ie Elementary School and Lanihuli and Wahinepee Streets.

Turn left on Naniloa Loop and go through the traffic circle, exiting right onto Po'ohaili Street.

Continue on Po'ohaili until you come to a sports field on your left; park next to it.

Trail Map

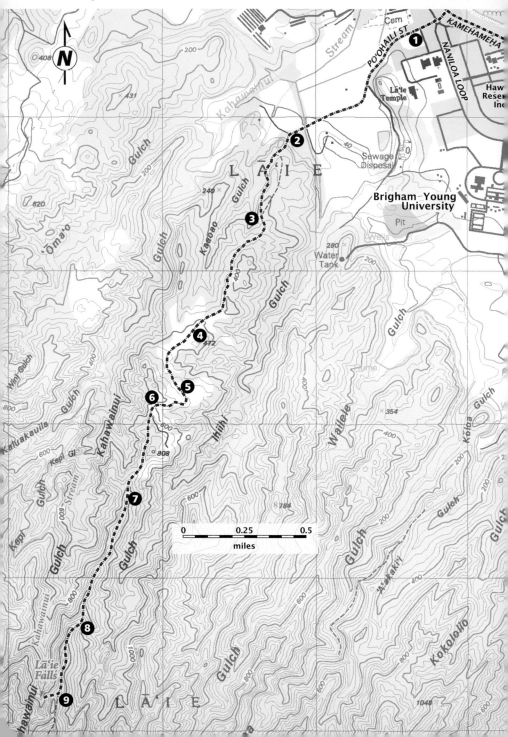

Trail Description

1. Begin the hike along Poʻohaili Street, passing the last of the residential buildings. When you reach a metal gate marked by a small trail sign, pass through it. Continue on this road, ignoring intersecting roads. Pass a green pumphouse on your right. Stay on this road as you cross over a bridge, where there is a second trail sign.

2. When you reach a signed junction in an overgrown, grassy area, pass over boulders to the left of a yellow gate, leaving the road as it veers right. There is a large trail map near the gate.

3. The route follows a rough dirt road. When the path forks, go left uphill (the right fork leads to an open area). As you ascend the eroded path, keep to the right to avoid spur trails. After passing through an arbor of distinctive ironwood trees, you enter an eroded open area.

4. Take careful note of the directions for sites 4, 5 and 6, because the trail is indistinct in the eroded sections. The trail narrows for a stretch, then crosses another open area, where you continue straight, avoiding a spur trail to the left.

5. The next open area is bounded by a fence line to your right in a vegetated area above the trail. Continue straight, avoiding a spur trail going up a bank on your right toward the fence line.

6. Continue straight until you reach a wooden fence post immediately to the right of the trail; a barbed wire fence angles uphill. Veer to the right to follow the trail as it parallels this fence line. The trail leaves the fence line and comes to another junction, where there is an unmarked steel pole. Take the right, more eroded, trail uphill. This stretch can be difficult in wet weather; it can also be confusing, because there are no trail signs. Be cautious.

7. About an hour from the start, you reach a forest of Cook pines. A distinct trail leads out of the forest.

8. The trail briefly descends and then skirts along side ridges. Strawberry guavas are abundant along this section. Watch your footing through the narrow parts with drop-offs.

9. When you arrive at a major fork, go right up the slight embankment, then descend to the Kahawainui Stream (the left fork continues to a summit). Be careful on the very rugged, steep steps. At the base, there are two waterfalls and a pool. Do not spend time in the gorge during or just after a heavy rainfall, because this area is known for flash floods. Enjoy these beautiful remote waterfalls, then retrace your steps to the trailhead.

The Mormon Temple, Brigham Young University and the Polynesian Cultural Center

Members of the The Church of Jesus Christ of Latter-Day Saints settled on O'ahu in 1864 and in 1919 built the Mormon Temple located near the town of Lā'ie. The public is welcome in the courtyard, but only members of the Mormon faith are permitted to enter the temple sanctuary.

Brigham Young University is also located near Lā'ie, as is the Polynesian Cultural Center. The center is located on 42 acres and creates a replica of ancient Polynesia, portraying life in the Marquesas, Tahiti, Fiji, Tonga, New Zealand and old Hawai'i. The elaborate show is the most popular tourist attraction on O'ahu and well worth the price of the ticket and the travel time to the northeast coast.

24. Kaunala and Pu'u o Mahuka Heiau

Map: USGS Waimea and Kahuku

Distance: 3 mile loop

Time: 3 hours

Rating: moderate

Elevation gain: 600 feet

Footwear and special equipment: trail shoes

Best time and season: all seasons

Distance from Waikīkī to trailhead: 46.5 miles

Hours of operation: open only on weekends and holidays, from daybreak to sunset

Highlights

This delightful walk has beautiful views of the North Shore. The trail winds up and down through gullies and follows a little-traveled four-wheel-drive road built over the colorful volcanic soil. Look closely, and you may see orchids on the roadside and, in the distance, flat-topped Mount Ka'ala ("fragrance"), the highest mountain on O'ahu. On the trail you can see a variety of plants, including the unusual-looking paperbark trees.

Access Map

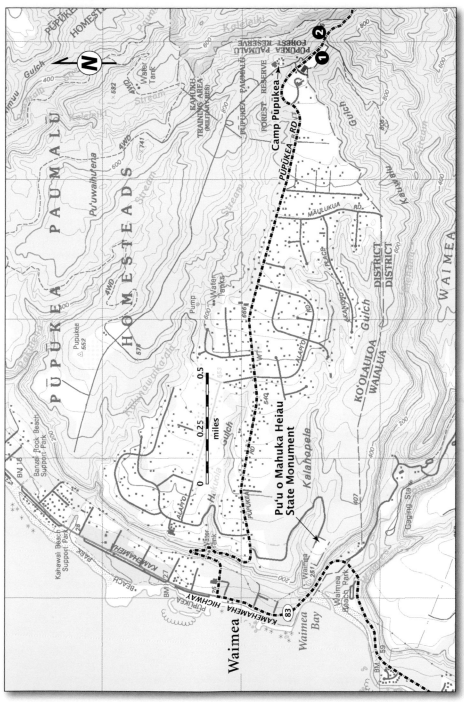

Access from Waikīkī to Trailhead

Take McCully Street *mauka* (toward the mountains) across the Lunalilo Freeway (H-1) and go left onto the H-1 westbound.

Stay on the H-1, passing the Pali (SR 61) and Likelike (SR 63) highways (the H-1 becomes the Queen Liliʻuokalani Freeway west of exit 19) until you reach the intersection with Veterans Memorial Freeway (H-2). Take exit 8A and drive to Wahiawā, where the freeway ends. Take exit 8 for Kamehameha Highway SR 80 northward toward Haleʻiwa.

Pass the Dole Plantation on the right. On the outskirts of Haleʻiwa, take the right fork for the Joseph P. Leong Highway (Haleʻiwa Bypass), which rejoins Kamehameha Highway

Puʻu o Mahuka Heiau (below)

(SR 83) north of town. Continue north, passing Waimea Bay and then the Waimea Falls Adventure Park on your right. Look for a Foodland Supermarket, a short drive past Waimea Bay, and turn right onto Pūpūkea Road. You will see a turnoff for the Puʻu o Mahuka Heiau 0.6 miles up the road (worth a visit after the hike, see page 158). Continue to the end of Pūpūkea Road and park on the road beside the Pūpūkea Boy Scout Camp.

Trail Description

1. To begin the Kaunala ("the plaiting") Trail, pass around the gate and sign in at the hunter check-in station on your left.

Puʻu o Mahuka Heiau (above)

2. The hike begins on the road, where you pass a sign that says "Pūpūkea Range; Government Property." Stay left. Shortly afterward, the road swings to the right; look for a trail sign for the Kaunala Trail.

3. Turn left onto a wide forest trail and leave the road behind (it will be your return route).

4. Note the directional sign indicating that the main trail goes right. For the next while, the trail crosses several streambeds as it switchbacks up and down gullies.

5. A spur trail on your left leads to a viewpoint.

6. When you reach another viewpoint, you have views of the ocean and the Kaunala Gulch.

7. Where the trail intersects with a four-wheel-drive road, turn right and ascend a long uphill.

8. Orchids are rare here, but if you look carefully you may spot some of these beautiful white and pink flowers on the side of the road

9. Continue to a flat, open area covered with red volcanic soil. This location offers the most spectacular view of Waimea Bay and, on a clear day, a view of the Waimea Mountains, including Mount Kaʻala, the tallest mountain on Oʻahu.

Trail Map

Puʻu o Mahuka Heiau (below)

10. Pass through a yellow gate to a T-junction. Turn right.

11. After you pass a sheltered picnic table, continue on the road until you close the loop, and then retrace your steps to the trailhead. If you have the time, drive back down the Pūpūkea Road until you reach the entrance to the Puʻu o Mahuka Heiau and visit this ancient Polynesian temple.

Kamehameha Schools and Bishop Estate

Born in 1831, Princess Bernice Pauahi, the great-granddaughter of King Kamehameha I, became the greatest benefactor of Hawai'ian youth. As a royal descendent, Bernice inherited nine percent of the total land of Hawai'i—lands that she bequeathed for the education and benefit of Hawai'ians. After her death in 1883, her husband, American businessman Charles Reed Bishop, managed her estate (Bishop Estate) and carried out her will. Kamehameha Schools now has three campuses and an additional 32 preschools dedicated to the education of Hawai'ian children. The area surrounding the Kaunala Trail is among the extensive lands still held by Bishop Estate.

Pu'u o Mahuka Heiau State Monument

It is part of Hawai'ian legend that this temple (its name means "hill of escape") was constructed by the *menehune*, the Hawai'ian little people, in a single night. The structure, likely originally built in the 1600s, consists of a low-walled, platform-type temple with two adjoining, smaller structures. According to oral history, in ancient times, this temple was used not just for worship but for human sacrifice

as well, and several accounts suggest that three of the men Captain George Vancouver sent ashore near here for water in 1793 were sacrificed at this site. Kamehameha I had his high priest conduct religious ceremonies at this *heiau* from 1795, when Kamehameha conquered O'ahu, until 1819, when the traditional religion was officially abolished. Today, the spiritual connection to the *heiau* remains. Offerings of many items (such as fruit, vegetables, rum and stones wrapped in ti leaves) are left here, demonstrating the spiritual importance of the temple among today's Hawai'ians.

Banzai Pipeline

'Ehukai Beach is the home of the Banzai Pipeline, one of the world's most famous surfing areas. Spectators crowd this beach to watch the surfers during competitions and when high winds create waves as high as 30 feet; the surf is most active in winter. To get there from the end of the Kaunala hike, exit Pūpūkea Road, turning right onto the Kamehameha Highway and continue northwest 1.2 miles to 'Ehukai Beach. Sunset Beach Elementary School is on your right across from limited beach parking on the left.

Plants to Look For

Paperbark tree

A member of the eucalyptus family—with the characteristic camphor odor—this tree, which can reach 100 feet in height, can be identified by its spongy, peeling, white bark and white, bottlebrush flowers. Native to Australia and vicinity, it can be invasive in wetland areas, often creating dense thickets.

'Ehukai Beach, site of the famous surfing area, the Banzai Pipeline (below)

25. Keālia and Kuaokalā Ridge

Map: USGS Ka'ena

Distance: 12 miles out and back, including the Kuaokalā Ridge loop

Time: 5 hours

Rating: moderate to difficult (ridge walk with steep slopes)

Elevation gain: 2000 feet

Footwear and special equipment: light hiking boots; bright clothing during hunting season

Best time and season: morning; winter, when it is cooler

Distance from Waikīkī to trailhead: 44 miles

Hours of operation: gate to Dillingham Airport is open from 7:00 AM to 6:00 PM daily

Highlights

Kuaokalā Ridge ("back of the sun") is the most spectacular trail in this guide, and this hike is the most challenging. From the ridge, there are views of the westerly tip of Oah'u as well as a view of the highest mountain on the island. Although the trail is not always well marked, the challenge of completing the loop is well worth the effort in map and terrain navigation.

Access from Waikīkī to Trailhead

Take McCully Street *mauka* (toward the mountains) across the Lunalilo Freeway (H-1) and immediately go left onto Dole Street, which you stay on for one block. Turn left onto Alexander Street and, where it ends, go right onto the H-1 on-ramp to merge onto the H-1 westbound.

Stay on the H-1, passing the Pali (SR 61) and Likelike (SR 63) highways (the H-1 becomes the Queen Liliʻuokalani Freeway west of exit 19) until you reach the intersection with the Veterans Memorial Freeway (H-2). Take exit 8A and drive to Wahiawā, where the freeway ends.

The roads in this area are not always well marked, and you may find yourself off course, but don't worry, because you won't be far off and the trip may be adventurous, especially if you happen to find yourself in the beautiful town of Haleʻiwa and then have to backtrack. Just remember, your route heads north and west to the end of the Farrington Highway on Kaʻena Point, the most westerly point on Oʻahu.

The best approach from Wahiawā is to go straight off the end of the H-2 (exit 9) onto Wilikina Drive (SR 99). After a merge, it becomes Kaukonahua Road (SR 803). It is about 13 miles from Wahiawā to Waialua.

As you approach Waialua, a set of flashing yellow lights marks a junction where you continue straight ahead, now on the Farrington Highway (SR 930). When you reach the traffic circle at Goodale Avenue, go halfway around it to stay on the Farrington Highway, headed for Mokuleia.

Stay on the Farrington Highway as it follows the ocean toward the trailhead at Dillingham Airport.

Pass beside a long green fence on the left and a sign for the skydiving school. On your right, you pass Mokuleia Beach Park, with its camping and picnic areas.

Note: The Keālia Trail provides week-round access to the Kuaokalā Ridge Loop without a permit. If possible, to begin in the relative cool of the morning, arrive in the area the day before the hike and stay at one of the delightful small towns on the North Shore or camp near the trailhead at Mokuleia Beach Park. Kuaokalā Ridge Loop is also accessible from Keaʻau Beach Park on the Farrington Highway, but you need a permit (see hike 30).

Access Map

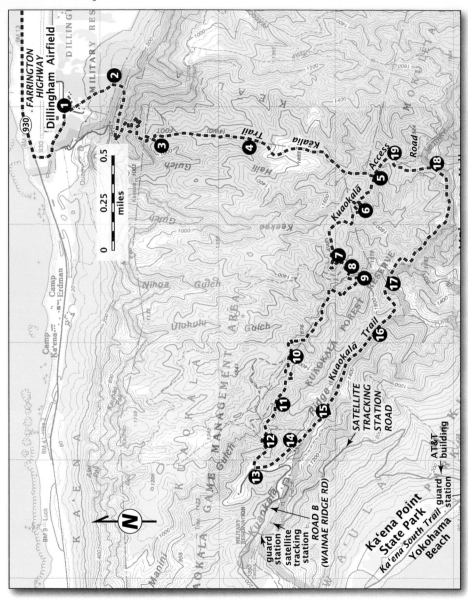

Pass the first gate into Dillingham Airport (on your left). Turn left through the second gate and look for the Keālia Trail sign.

There is a second trail sign as you drive into the airport. Follow the paved road for 0.4 miles and look for another trail sign and, on your left, a public parking area.

Trail Description

1.   From the parking lot, cross the road and pass between the yellow posts. Walk *mauka* (toward the mountains) on deteriorating pavement, passing an old airport structure to your right. Now on a dirt road, continue through a grove of koa hoale trees to a fork in the road. Take the right fork, following the arrow.

2.   At a subsequent fork, go left and through an opening in a low, green fence, where there is a sign for the Keālia ("salt encrustation") Trail; a warning sign from the military cautions hikers to stay on the trail. The trail begins with a series of switchbacks as it winds up this northwestern ridge of the

GPS Data Table

If you bring a GPS (Global Positioning System), waypoint data on the following page can assist you on this trail as the route is not well marked. However, the GPS data is only accurate to 30 meters (about 100 feet) and GPS data may not be reliable in areas of dense tree cover.

Trail Map

GPS Data Table

Site # on Map	Latitude	Longitude	Site # on Map	Latitude	Longitude
1	N 21° 33.8112'	W 158° 14.2578'	9	N 21° 33.4044'	W 158° 13.0470'
2	N 21° 33.5478'	W 158° 14.0754'	10	N 21° 33.3558'	W 158° 13.2768'
3	N 21° 33.4806'	W 158° 13.9764'	11	N 21° 33.4872'	W 158° 13.3308'
4	N 21° 33.2070'	W 158° 13.5198'	12	N 21° 33.3282'	W 158° 13.3116'
5	N 21° 33.1698'	W 158° 13.4076'	13	N 21° 33.6390'	W 158° 13.6788'
6	N 21° 33.0264'	W 158° 12.7578'	14	N 21° 33.6978'	W 158° 13.9176'
8	N 21° 33.2352'	W 158° 12.8202'	15	N 21° 33.7872'	W 158° 14.1270'

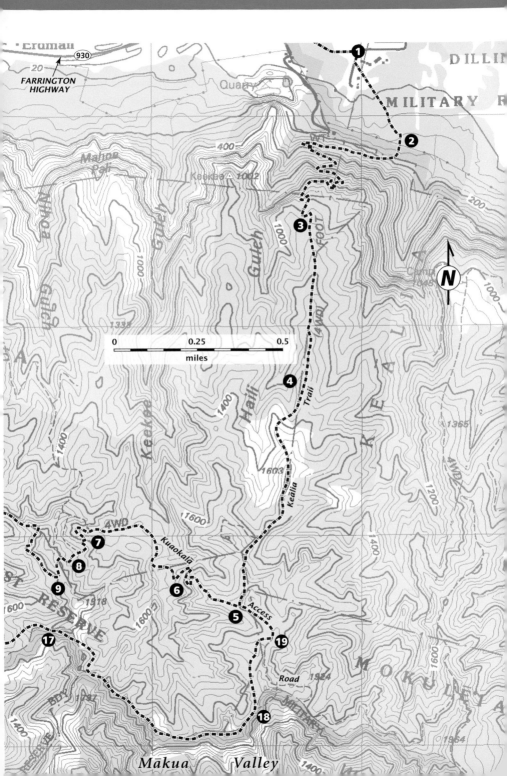

Waiʻanae Range. Look down to see a deep green pool of water in an old quarry. The ascent is steep but relatively short, so you can expect to finish the steepest part in about an hour. As you climb up the ridge, spectacular views of the North Shore and the rolling surf appear.

3.   At the 18th switchback, the main trail leads to a picnic table and shelter. Follow the dirt road uphill. At the first junction, by an old fence, keep right. For the way back, note the sign identifying the Keālia Trail. Pass through an open gate and into a fenced area. Continue through a grassy area.

4.   Pass a water tank on your left and continue on through an area of introduced pine trees. A view of the ocean awaits after a climb up a long slope. A sign for the Kuaokalā Public Hunting Area stands near a spur trail to the left. Stay right, ascending on the main road.

5.   At a signed T-junction, go right to begin the Kuaokalā loop. The road to the left is your return trail. The Kuaokalā Access Road intersects several times with the old road; stay left at each junction.

6.   When you reach a Y-intersection, go left uphill on the more traveled road. Continue for about a mile through a heavily forested area, shady and without views.

7. Go left at a T-junction, staying on the more traveled road.

8. Look for a directional sign, where you go left. You soon reach a viewpoint overlooking the North Shore.

9. Continue along the red dirt road to another fork, where again you again stay left; the overgrown right fork goes up steeply over red soil between the pines. Stay on the road when it veers sharply right; to the left of the curve is a clearing, not an intersecting road.

10. When you reach a cleared area to the right of a fence line where there is a sign regarding public hunting, you can either bear left on the rough and badly eroded section of the old road or remain on the main, more-traveled road, which is longer. In wet weather, you may want to remain on the new road, because the shortcut on the old road is becoming severely rutted.

11. Rejoin the main road and go left.

12. Soon you pass a hunter information sign and utility installation. The dirt road ends, and you are now on a paved surface. Ascend on this road to a T-intersection. Look to your left at the intersection to see the Kuaokalā Trail sign.

13. Starting at the trail sign, begin the next leg of the hike on a narrow dirt path on the hillside.

14. At the first intersection, go left on a dirt road along the ridge.

15. Pass a picnic shelter on your right. From the shelter to the top of the small rise, the route is slightly overgrown. At the top, you will be back on a well-defined dirt road. The dirt road cuts just below the ridge. Below you can see the guardhouse, where hikers doing this route from the south present their permits, and also an AT&T building.

16. The road becomes quite overgrown as it dips into a small ravine. Continue straight up toward the ridge, passing an

intersection on your left. Look for an arrow marking the route and go left on the narrow dirt road up the ridge, where there is a second directional arrow. Where the road ends, ascend along the ridge, where there are narrow, steep sections, sometimes along a trail and at times over eroded areas. Be cautious in wet weather. At another arrow, bear right. Continue alongside the ridge as the trail crosses an open area, then climbs steeply through vegetation. When you reach a distinctive eroded knob, veer left and steeply down about 10 feet on the eroded and gullied trail.

17. The trail comes out onto the southerly side of the ridge, where you soon have a view of the Mākua Valley and the steep walls of Ohikilolo ("scooped-out brains") Ridge. The buildings in the valley are part of the military installation. You then emerge from the vegetated area onto another eroded area with views of the North Shore.

18. Scramble down steep, red rock slabs, using caution in wet conditions, down a gully and then climb steeply up a dirt path to an intersection and a lookout. The less distinct trail to the right leads to the Kuaokalā Access Road. On a clear day, you can see the flat-topped, 4025-foot Mount Kaʻala ("fragrance"), the highest peak on Oʻahu. Turn left away from the ridge and descend on a wide dirt road.

19. When you come to a junction, continue straight onto the signed Kuaokalā Access Road. A little water tank is to your left. You complete the loop when you come to the intersection with the Keālia Trail (location 5 on the map). Turn right to retrace your steps to the Dillingham Airfield.

Plants To Look For

Wiliwili tree (Hawai'ian coral tree, tiger's claw)

This endemic small tree of the leeward dry forests has heart-shaped, leathery leaves in groups of three. After dropping its leaves for the summer dry season, it produces unusual curved flowers. Blooms are usually orange, but can also be red, white, yellow or greenish. Hawai'ians used the wood for canoe outriggers and surfboards. The name wiliwili ("repeatedly twisted") refers to the seedpods, each typically containing one to three red seeds, which are strung to form leis. At this writing, this tree (along with several closely related ornamental species) is being threatened by a tiny African wasp that destroys the leaves. Look for this tree on the ascent from Dillingham Airfield.

26. Ka'ena Point North

Map: USGS Ka'ena

Distance: 5 miles out and back

Time: 3.5 hours

Rating: easy

Elevation gain: none

Footwear and special equipment: walking shoes; this hike is entirely out in the open, so bring a sun hat, sunscreen and plenty of water; binoculars to view wildlife; pick up a copy of *A Nature Walk to Ka'ena Point* at the Division of Land and Natural Resources (see p. 11)

Best time and season: winter or spring, when it is cooler; fall and winter are best for wildlife (see hike 30)

Distance from Waikīkī to trailhead: approx. 51 miles

Highlights

This hike shows you the pounding surf of the North Shore and, in the winter, gives you a chance to see the Laysan albatross and humpback whales. It takes you through an ecosystem that is one of the best examples of coastal lowland dunes.

Access from Waikīkī to Trailhead

Take McCully Street *mauka* (toward the mountains)

across the Lunalilo Freeway
(H-1) and immediately go
left onto Dole Street, which
you stay on for one block.
Turn left onto Alexander
Street and, where it ends, go
right onto the H-1 onramp
to merge onto the H-1
westbound.

Stay on the H-1, passing
the Pali (SR 61) and
Likelike (SR 63) highways
(the H-1 becomes the
Queen Lili'uokalani Freeway
west of exit 19) until you
reach the intersection with
the Veterans Memorial
Freeway (H-2). Take exit 8A
and drive to Wahiawā,
where the freeway ends.

The roads in this area are not
always well marked, and you
may find yourself off course,
but don't worry, because
you won't be far off and the
trip may be adventurous,
especially if you happen to
find yourself in the beautiful
town of Hale'iwa and then
have to backtrack. Just
remember, your route heads
north and west to the end of
the Farrington Highway on
Ka'ena Point, the most
westerly point on O'ahu.

The best approach from
Wahiawā is to go straight off
the end of the H-2 (exit 9)
onto Wilikina Drive (SR 99).
After a merge, it becomes
Kaukonahua Road (SR 803).
It is about 13 miles from
Wahiawā to Waialua.

Notes: The best way to do this hike is to walk from Ka'ena Point State Park in the south (see hike 30) to the North Shore and arrange for transportation at the other end. TheBus does not service either end of the Ka'ena Point Trail.

To protect the wildlife at the point, please do not bring any pets on this hike.

Ka'ena means "the heat," so be prepared to walk in the sun for the entire route. Be cautious when near the ocean, because the waves can be fierce (on rare occasions to 50 feet in height!), and a rogue wave could sweep you out to sea.

Never turn your back on the sea when you are close to the water.

Access Map

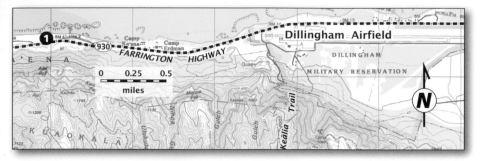

As you approach Waialua, a set of flashing yellow lights marks a junction where you continue straight ahead, now on the Farrington Highway (SR 930). When you reach the traffic circle at Goodale Avenue, go halfway around it to stay on the Farrington Highway, headed for Mokuleia.

Once you pass Mokuleia, the ocean is on your right. Pass Dillingham Airport, continuing along the coast a further 7 miles to the end of the pavement. Park off the paved road and do not leave any valuables in your vehicle. A local travel writer advises leaving the doors and trunk of your car unlocked, with nothing in the vehicle.

Trail Description

1. Step around the gate and follow the old railroad bed or one of the parallel dirt roads. The route crosses sand dunes and passes delightful ocean coves. The Wai'anae Ridge rises up to your left, and the ocean with its spectacular breakers is on your right. As you walk toward the point, there are several spur trails; ignore them.

2. About halfway to Ka'ena Point, you cross a barrier and a sign for the Ka'ena Point Natural Area Reserve, which was designated for the protection of nesting birds, such as the Laysan albatross, and rare coastal plants, so be sure to stay well back from the nests and leave the plants undamaged. By staying on the designated trail, you help protect this sensitive dune environment. Along with various seabirds, humpback whales and Hawai'ian monk seals can sometimes be spotted from the shore here.

Part of the old rail and highway rights-of-way (above)

Trail Map

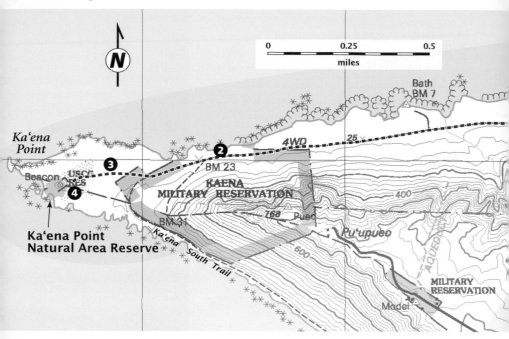

3. Look for a distinctive large rock on the sea side of the trail. This culturally significant site is called Leina ka 'uhane ("leaping of souls rock").

4. Turn around at the lighthouse and retrace your steps back to the trailhead.

Leina ka 'uhane

According to native Hawai'ian tradition, this sacred spot is one of several throughout the Hawai'ian Islands where the soul departs from the earth for the next world. Along the path near this site, you will see many spiritual offerings set out on rocks. Take care not to disturb them.

Mongooses

You may see animal traps at Ka'ena Point. They are set to trap mongooses. Native to India, the small Asian mongoose was brought to Jamaica to control the rats in the sugar plantations in 1872 and from there to Hawai'i in the 1880s. However, because rats are most active by night, whereas the mongoose hunts mostly by day, it failed to do

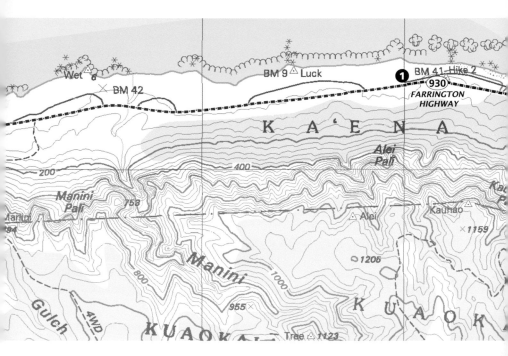

much about the rat problem. What is worse, this hungry carnivore also devours insects, frogs, lizards and birds, and its introduction has been very hard on native Hawai'ian species.

History of the Trail Route

This trail follows part of the route of the Oahu Railway, constructed in the late 1890s to carry sugarcane. By 1947, rail transportation had been replaced by truck hauling. In the early 1950s, the Farrington Highway was built around the point. It eventually eroded, and, in the early 1970s, plans to build a modern highway around the point were rejected by Hawai'ians because of environmental concerns. To help protect the sensitive dune environment from abuse by offroaders, Ka'ena Point Natural Area Reserve was designated in 1983, and it was later expanded.

Plants to Look For

Naio (false sandalwood, bastard sandalwood)

This widespread, sun-loving shrub or small tree has small, trumpet-shaped, white or lavender flowers and slender, dull green leaves that look slightly twisted. The plant bears soft, white, half-inch fruits. Naio got its alternative names because it was tried as a substitute for true sandalwood, which is renowned for its fragrant, attractive wood and essential oils. In ancient times, naio's hard, yellow wood was used in home construction.

Beach naupaka (half flower, naupaka kahakai)

This sturdy, mounding, indigenous evergreen shrub of dry coastal places has large, smooth-edged leaves and white flowers that mature to fleshy, white fruit. In the unusual flower design, it appears that the top half of the flower is missing, leaving just the lower petals. A closely related plant of higher elevations has a flower of opposite design. Naupaka is an important dune stabilizer.

'Ohai

A low, spreading, endangered, endemic shrub or small tree of low-elevation dry areas, 'ohai has compound leaves and elongated, pealike, red or orange flowers.

Pōhinahina (beach vitex)

Small, purple flowers, which are used in leis, decorate this low-growing, clump-forming, indigenous shrub of coastal areas. This important dune colonizer helps hold the sand in place. The fragrant, round or oval leaves are used medicinally.

Malina (sisal plant)

A tall, dryland agave species from Mexico, sisal has spikes up to 30 feet tall. The plant was brought to Hawai'i as a fiber crop and was used to make rope, but sisal has now mostly been replaced by synthetic materials.

Beach naupaka

Malina

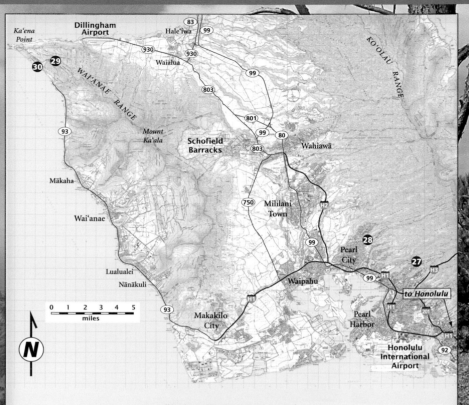

27. 'Aiea Loop: Keaīwa Heiau State Park

Highlights

A variety of tropical plants and trees, including swamp mahogany and paperbark trees, grow in this typical low-to-middle-elevation moist forest and wet shrubland habitat. There are also beautiful views of the ocean. The hike is on a well-maintained trail with an excellent camping and picnic spot near the

Map: USGS Kāne'ohe and Waipahu

Distance: 4.3 mile loop

Time: 2.5 hours

Rating: moderate

Elevation gain: 900 feet

Footwear and special equipment: trail shoes

Best time and season: all seasons

Distance from Waikīkī to trailhead: approx. 16 miles

Hours of operation: 7:00 AM to 7:45 PM from April 1 to Labor Day, closing at 6:45 PM the rest of the year

Access Map

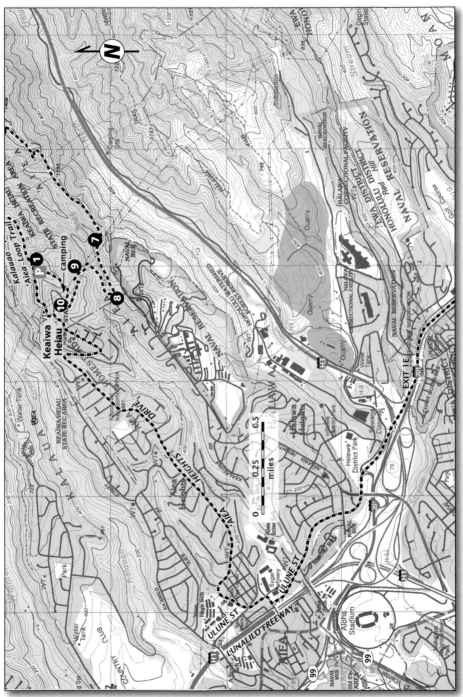

Trail Map

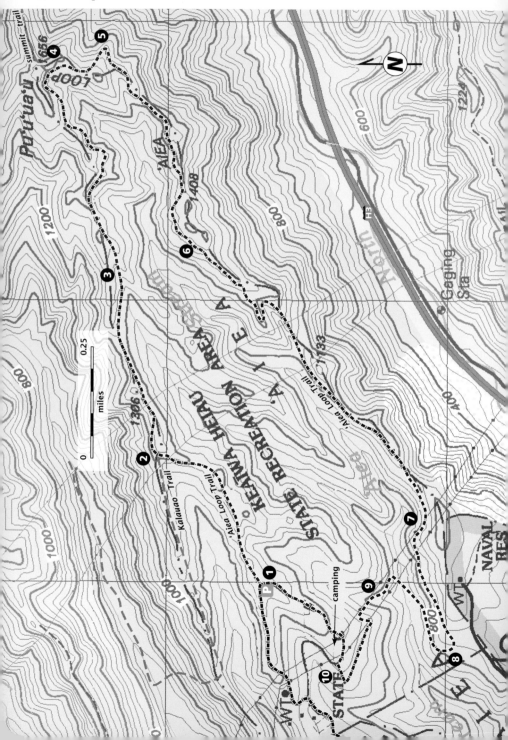

trailhead. Keaīwa Heiau, the remains of an ancient Hawai'ian temple, is near the trailhead. On the last part of this hike, when you have views of the gullies, look for a grove of trees with pale green leaves, the state tree, kuku'i.

Access from Waikīkī to Trailhead

Follow driving directions carefully, because the access to 'Aiea Heights Drive is easy to miss, and the exits from the H-1 and H-201 can be confusing.

Take McCully Street *mauka* (toward the mountains) across the Lunalilo Freeway (H-1) and go left onto the H-1 westbound. After passing the Likelike Highway (SR 63), move to the left lane and take exit 19B (at Middle Street) to the left onto the Moanalua Freeway (H-201/SR 78). As you go up Red Hill, take exit 1E (Halawa–Stadium). From the long ramp, continue straight onto Ulune Street. Turn right at the T-intersection with 'Aiea Heights Drive, which soon takes a corner to the left and then curves to the right through the following intersection. Continue on this ascending, circuitous street to Keaīwa Heiau State Park. Drive past the *heiau* on your left and pull into the parking lot at the road's highest point.

Trail Description

1. The trail begins near the water tank adjacent to the parking lot. Beneath a canopy of eucalyptus trees, the path is rough at first, with roots underfoot. Soon the trail intersects the power line for the first time. There are beautiful views of the ocean and the adjacent valley as the trail heads up the ridge.

2. When you reach a junction that leads off to the left (the Kalauao Trail), stay on the wider loop trail. You soon meet with the power line a second time.

3. The trail narrows, and you reach an open ridge overlooking the Pacific Ocean and Pearl Harbor.

4. Cross the head of the valley, where there is an indistinct trail to the left that climbs a further 2 miles to the crest of Ko'olau Range. Keep to the right.

5. Soon you reach a bench with a view; the H-3 freeway lies below. The trail then follows the southern ridge of the valley and begins descending.

6. A few minutes down the trail and on your right on the side of the gully is the wreckage of a B-24J four-engine Liberator bomber that crashed on its maiden trip, from California to Australia, after taking off from Hickam Field in 1944; all 10 crewmembers died.

Discovered in 1993, the plane is barely visible. Over the past six decades, soil has sloughed down the hill covering the wreck, and parts have been removed for museum use.

7. When you again reach the power line that stretches across the valley, you will find ironwood trees and Cook pines. Avoid the spur routes before once again crossing under a pair of power lines. At a spur trail to the left, keep right, following a sign that indicates the correct direction.

8. Where another spur trail goes off to the left, go right, following the sign "Keaīwa Heiau Loop." The terrain becomes a little rougher as you descend to the creek. This intermittent stream may be dry in a drought season.

9.   There are two further crossings under the power lines as the trail switches back and forth. The path, with its beautiful red soil surface, becomes level and wide.

10.   You come out near the camping and picnic spot on 'Aiea Heights Drive. Take the steps up from the camping area and walk about 0.3 miles along the paved road back to the parking area.

The Keaīwa Heiau

The Keaīwa ("mysterious") Heiau healing site is near the park entrance. The 600-year-old temple was once used by *kahuna lapa'au* (Hawai'ian healers), and what remains of it today continues to be an important sacred site for native Hawai'ians. An arboretum of medicinal plants has been established in the surrounding area. Some of the herbs are still used by local residents.

Further Information: *'Aiea Loop Trail and Keaīwa Heiau* is one of a number of guides available from the Moanalua Gardens Foundation, 1352 Pineapple Place, Honolulu, HI 96819; phone: (808) 839-5334; website: http://www.mgf-hawaii.org/.

Plants to Look For

kuku'i (p. 126)

Keaiwa Heiau

28. Waimano

Highlights

The Waimano ("many waters") Trail is a peaceful, easy walk that offers shade along the route. During the wet season, the Waimano Stream is a delight, with the water creating small rapids and pools. In the dry season, there may be little water; instead, you can enjoy the shaded valley and its beautiful streambed of boulders.

Map: USGS Waipahu

Distance: 2 miles round trip

Time: 1 hour

Rating: easy

Elevation gain: 300 feet

Footwear and special equipment: trail shoes

Best time and season: all seasons

Distance from Waikīkī to trailhead: approx. 16 miles

Access Map

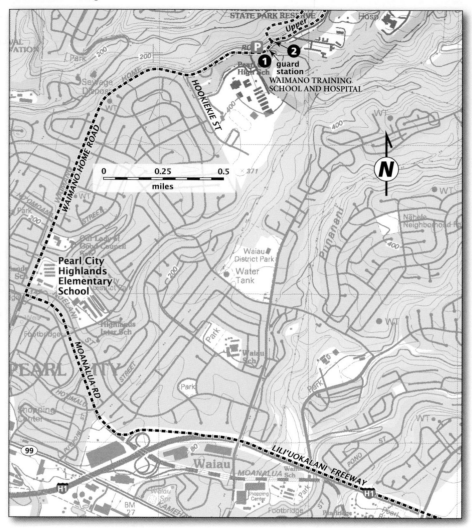

Access from Waikīkī to Trailhead

The following approach, although not the fastest, is the simplest for visitors new to Honolulu.

Take McCully Street *mauka* (toward the mountains) across the Lunalilo Freeway (H-1) and immediately go left onto Dole Street, which you stay on for one block. Turn left onto Alexander Street and,

where it ends, go right onto the H-1 on-ramp to merge onto the H-1 westbound.

Continue on the H-1 westbound, passing the Honolulu International Airport and Aloha Stadium exits (the H-1 becomes the Queen Lili'uokalani Freeway west of exit 19) and take exit 10 (West Pearl City–Waimalu).

At the end of the exit ramp, turn right onto Moanalua Road. Where it ends, go right onto Waimano Home Road and pass Pearl City Highlands Elementary School (on your right).

Continue on Waimano Home Road until you pass Hookiekie Street and the Waimano Training School and Hospital.

Park on the left shoulder of the road, just before the guard station, near the Pearl City Cultural Center.

Trail Description

1. The trailhead is immediately beyond the gate at the guard station and to the left of the fence. The trail begins through a grove of swamp mahogany.

Trail Map

2. Continue along the fence until you reach a T-junction. Take the right fork, which is marked "Upper Waimano Trail" (the left fork will be your return route). Look for Java plum trees along this trail.

3. At the junction about 0.5 miles out on the trail, stay left (the right fork is a spur trail).

4. Stay on the main trail as it follows an old irrigation system for a short section. The tunnel is passable but not pleasant because of the refuse in it.

5. At a Y-junction, take the left fork (the right fork is the continuation of the Upper Waimano Trail, which carries on a further 4 miles to the crest of the Ko'olau Ridge). At the next junction, stay on the main trail (the small trail continues up the valley).

6. The trail drops down and follows the Waimano Creek, which may be dry in some seasons. This section has a few spur trails, so remain on the main trail. As you head back to the trailhead, there are beautiful views of the ridge to the north.

7. Soon you are on a wide, grassy path. When you reach the junction with the Upper Waimano Trail, you close the loop. Stay right and continue back to the trailhead.

Feral Pigs
Feral (wild) pigs are found in middle elevations of O'ahu, such as the Waimano area, where local residents hunt them. The Polynesians introduced pigs to the Hawai'ian Islands as an important source of food. These smallish pigs eventually inbred with the larger pigs imported by Europeans. Initially kept contained, they escaped and became wild. Their habit of digging vegetation and worms damages and kills the natural vegetation, causing significant environmental problems.

Plants to Look For

Christmas berry, hau, Java plum tree, strawberry guava and swamp mahogany (p. 144)

Hau (sea hibiscus)

An indigenous tree species of hibiscus that dominates valleys and streamsides, hau is often found in dense stands with intertwined trunks. Within a single day, one of the three-inch-wide, dark-centered, flowers opens yellow, becomes orangy bronze and then closes and drops. The wood has traditionally been used for canoe outriggers and to make a variety of implements, and the bark fibers have been employed for making ropes and bags.

Christmas berry (Brazilian peppertree)

This invasive, weedy, small tree from South America flourishes in pastures and moist areas. It is named for its bright red berries, which ripen in winter and have a peppery fragrance.

Strawberry guava

Recognized by its small, red fruit that tastes a little like strawberry, shiny leaves and smooth bark with patches, the strawberry guava is an invasive shrub or small tree from Brazil that often grows in tight thickets.

Java plum tree

This South Asian import, which can exceed 50 feet in height, bears soft, edible, elongated, olive-sized, dark purple fruit. The fruit matures in the summer, and in winter, you often see the trail covered with the fallen fruit.

29. Kuaokalā Ridge Loop

Highlights

Kuaokalā ("back of the sun") Ridge is the most spectacular trail in this guide. It skirts the ridge above the most westerly point of O'ahu, with amazing views of the ocean and the mountain ridges. The trail is not always well marked, but this difficulty is well compensated by the rewards of this hike.

Access from Waikīkī to Trailhead

Take McCully Street *mauka* (toward the mountains) across the Lunalilo Freeway (H-1) and immediately go left

Map: USGS Ka'ena

Distance: 5.5 mile loop

Time: 3.5 to 4 hours

Rating: moderate to difficult (ridge walk with steep slopes)

Elevation gain: 600 feet

Footwear: light hiking boots; bright clothing during hunting season

Best time and season: winter, when it is cooler

Distance from Waikīkī to Trailhead: approx. 44 miles

Permits and hours of operation: permit required from State Division of Forestry and Wildlife (see p. 11)

Note: Kuaokalā Ridge Loop is once more accessible from the south via Kea'au Beach Park on the Farrington Highway. The military had closed this access through the Makua Military Reservation following September 11, 2001, but it was reopened in 2004, subject to acquiring a permit. Do not hike off the trail into the Mākua Valley, which is used as a military range.

Caution: The route goes over a narrow saddle with steep drop-offs

Access Map

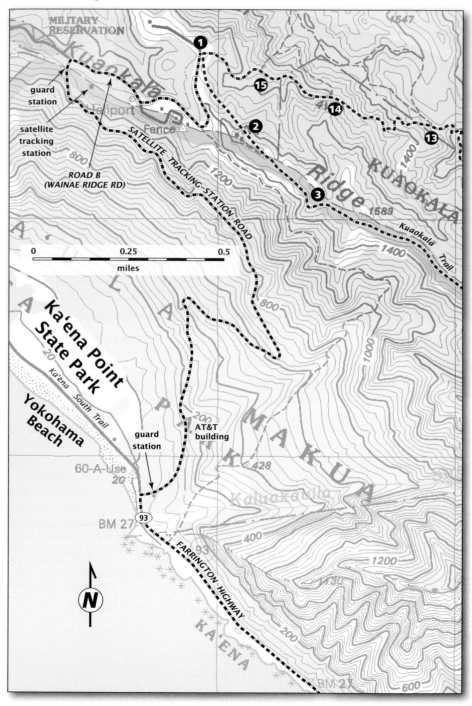

onto Dole Street, which you stay on for one block. Turn left onto Alexander Street and, where it ends, go right onto the H-1 on-ramp to merge onto the H-1 westbound.

Drive to the end of the H-1, avoiding exits for the Pali (SR 61) and Likelike (SR 63) highways and the John A. Burns (H-3) and Veterans Memorial (H-2) freeways. Be especially careful through the spaghetti of intersecting routes near Pearl City; follow the signs for Wai'anae.

Soon after the exit for Makakilo City, the H-1 ends and becomes the Farrington Highway (SR 93). Pass the Kō Olina Golf Course on your left, and soon the highway begins to skirt the ocean. Pass the towns of Nānākuli, Lualualei, the larger center of Wai'anae and then Mākaha. Shortly after leaving the town of Mākaha, look for a point of interest with an interpretive sign on your left; Kaneana Cave, on the opposite side of

the highway, is an interesting site to visit after your hike. As you near the Ka'ena Point State Park entrance at Yokohama Bay, turn right onto Satellite Tracking Station Road, stopping at the kiosk to give your permit to the guard and pick up your day pass.

Drive up the paved access road for about 2 miles. Use caution in wet weather, when this road can become slick.

When you reach the top, stop at the second guard station and wait to be let through. At the T-intersection, take Road B (Wainae Ridge Road) to the right and proceed past the satellite tracking station. Keep left at the next fork to bypass the administration buildings on your right.

Pass another intersection and continue straight; you soon pass through an open gate. Park in the dirt clearing on your right immediately after you pass a paved road that diverges to your right. (If you

Trail Map

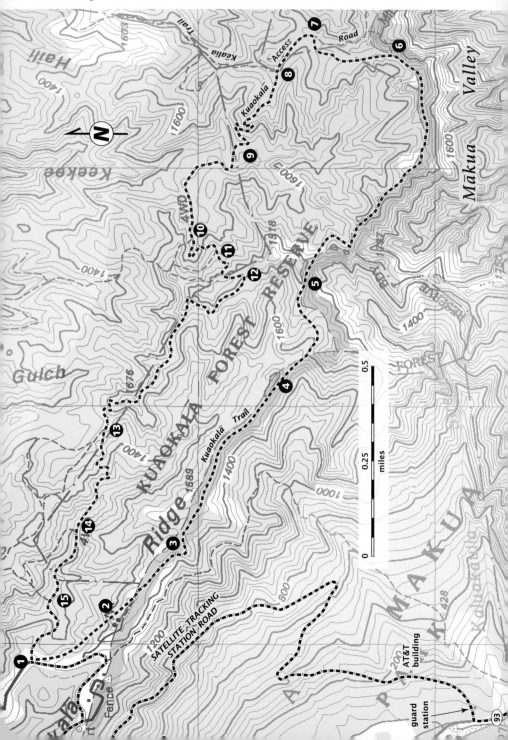

miss it, the main road soon ends at some more buildings.)

Trail Description

First, a note on keeping on the trail. Unlike many O'ahu trails, this one is not well signed. The first time we hiked Kuaokalā Ridge (clockwise), we lost the trail on the eroded sections of the ridge and turned back without completing the loop.

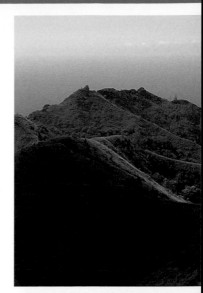

We recommend going counterclockwise (as shown in this trail description), because it's easier to stay on the route. Once you drop down from the ridge onto the all-wheel drive roads, the old road intersects with the new road at a number of forks. The route generally follows the old road; just keep left at each intersection. We found the route over the roads relatively easy to follow.

Remain on the trail, especially along the ridge, because the Mākua Valley to the south is used as a military range.

1. To begin, walk back the few hundred feet to the paved road that intersected on your right as you drove in (it is your return route). At this intersection, look for the signed Kuaokalā trailhead at the edge of the paved road (now on your left). Starting at the trail sign, begin on a narrow dirt path on the hillside.

2. At the first intersection, go left on a dirt road along the ridge.

Eucalyptus trees line the trail as you climb up to site 6 on the map. (below)

3. Pass a picnic shelter on your right. From the shelter to the top of the small rise, the trail is slightly overgrown. At the top you will be back on a well-defined dirt road. The dirt road cuts just below the ridge. Below you will see the guardhouse where you submitted your permit and the AT&T building you drove past.

4. The road becomes quite overgrown as it dips into a small ravine; continue straight up toward the ridge, passing an intersection on your left. Look for an arrow marking the route and go left on the

narrow dirt road up the ridge, where there is a second directional arrow. Where the road ends, ascend along the ridge, where there are narrow, steep sections. Be cautious in wet weather. At another arrow, bear right. Continue alongside the ridge as the trail crosses an open area, then climbs steeply through vegetation. When you reach a distinctive eroded knob, veer left and steeply down about 10 feet on the eroded and gullied trail.

5. The trail comes out onto the southerly side of the ridge, where you soon have a view of the Mākua Valley and the steep walls of Ohikilolo ("scooped-out brains") Ridge. The buildings in the valley are part of the military installation. You then emerge onto another eroded area with views of the North Shore.

6. Scramble down steep, red rock slabs, using caution in wet conditions, down a gully and then climb steeply up a dirt path to an intersection and a lookout. The less distinct trail to the right leads to the Kuaokalā Access Road. On a clear day, you can see the flat-topped, 4025-foot Mount Kaʻala ("fragrance"), the highest peak on Oʻahu. Turn left away from the ridge and descend on a wide dirt road.

7. When you come to a junction, continue straight onto the signed Kuaokalā Access Road. A little water tank is to your left.

8. At the T-junction with the Keālia Trail, keep left, staying on the main road. (The Keālia Trail leads down to Dillingham Airfield—see hike 25.) Avoid a spur trail to your left, keeping on the main road. The Kuaokalā Access Road intersects several times with the old road; stay left at each junction.

9. When you reach a Y-intersection, go left uphill on the more traveled road. Continue for about a mile through a heavily forested area, shady and without views.

10. Go left at a T-junction, staying on the more traveled road.

11. Look for a directional sign, where you go left. You soon reach a viewpoint overlooking the North Shore.

12. Continue along the red dirt road to another fork, where again you again stay left. (The overgrown right fork goes up steeply over red soil between the pines.) Stay on the road when it veers sharply right; to the left of the curve is a clearing, not an intersecting road.

13. When you reach a cleared area to the right of a fence line where there is a sign regarding public hunting, you can either bear left on the rough and badly eroded section of the old road or remain on the main, more-traveled road, which is longer. In wet weather you may want to remain on the new road, because the shortcut on the old road is becoming severely rutted.

14. Rejoin the main road and go left.

15. Soon you pass a hunter information sign and utility installation. The dirt road ends, and you are now on a paved surface. Ascend on this road back to the parking area.

Kaneana Cave

Kaneana Cave is located just north of the town of Mākaha. This culturally significant feature was created by wave action when ocean levels were much higher. It is the legendary home of *Nanue,* the shark man, and it was inhabited by the ancestors of today's Hawai'ians.

30. Kaʻena Point South

Map: USGS Kaʻena

Distance: 5 miles out and back

Time: 3.5 hours

Rating: easy

Elevation gain: none

Footwear and special equipment: walking shoes; this hike is entirely out in the open, so bring a sun hat, sunscreen and plenty of water; binoculars to view wildlife; flashlight for the cave; pick up a copy of *A Nature Walk to Kaʻena Point* at the Division of Land and Natural Resources (see p. 11)

Best time and season: winter or spring, when it is cooler; fall and winter are best for wildlife

Distance from Waikīkī to trailhead: approx. 45 miles

Highlights

This hike follows along the seacoast of rugged lava formations, with spectacular arches and tide pools. It is one of the most enjoyable walks on Oʻahu. There are caves used by the early Polynesians and awe-inspiring cliffs. As a bonus, you may see whales, monk seals and the rare Laysan albatross.

Access Map

Access from Waikīkī to Trailhead

Take McCully Street *mauka* (toward the mountains) across the Lunalilo Freeway (H-1) and immediately go left onto Dole Street, which you stay on for one block. Turn left onto Alexander Street and, where it ends, go right onto the H-1 onramp to merge onto the H-1 westbound.

Notes: Providing you can arrange transportation, we recommend starting with this hike and continuing onward from Ka'ena Point to the north trailhead near Dillingham Airport (see hike 26). Neither trailhead is served by TheBus.

To protect the wildlife at the point, please do not bring any pets on this hike.

Ka'ena means "the heat," so be prepared to walk in the sun for the entire route. Be cautious when near the ocean, because the waves can be fierce (on rare occasions to 50 feet in height!), and a rogue wave could sweep you out to sea.

Never turn your back on the sea when you are close to the water.

Trail Map

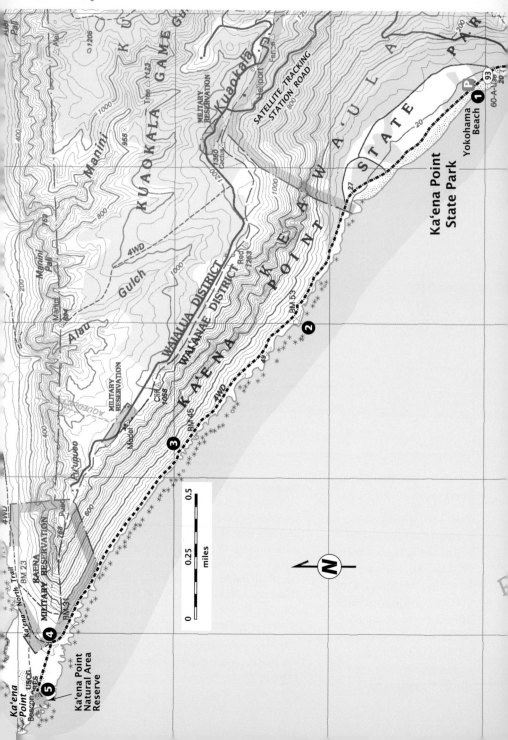

Drive to the end of the H-1, avoiding exits for the Pali (SR 61) and Likelike (SR 63) highways and the John A. Burns (H-3) and Veterans Memorial (H-2) freeways. Be especially careful through the spaghetti of intersecting routes near Pearl City; follow the signs for Wai'anae.

Soon after the exit for Makakilo City, the H-1 ends and becomes the Farrington Highway (SR 93). Pass the Ko Olina Golf Course on your left, and soon the highway begins to skirt the ocean. Pass the towns of Nānākuli, Lualualei, the larger center of Wai'anae and then Mākaha. Shortly after leaving the town of Mākaha, look for a point of interest with an interpretive sign on your left; Kaneana Cave, on the opposite side of the highway, is an interesting site to visit after your hike (see hike 29). Continue to the Ka'ena Point State Park entrance and park near the restrooms. Because of the risk of vandalism, it is best not to park at the actual trailhead.

Trail Description

1. Walk on the road past Yokohama Beach until the dirt road ends and the trail begins. The trail follows an old road and railway bed that once passed around Ka'ena Point, connecting the leeward (west) and north sides of the island.

2. In the first half mile of the hike, look for two blowholes in the lava formations, locally called Mutt and Jeff. Jeff spurts a fine mist, and Mutt sends out a lower spout of water. At high tide, they can be fun to watch.

3. Approximately 45 minutes from the start, the trail passes a deep cave immediately to your right. Look for the cave entrance near the trail washout. It is generally considered safe to explore. After exploring the cave, carefully traverse the section of eroded trail.

4. As you approach Ka'ena Point, you can see a lighthouse. You soon enter Ka'ena Point Natural Area Reserve (see hike 29), which was designated for the protection of nesting birds, such as the Laysan albatross, and rare coastal plants, so be sure to stay well back from the nests and leave the plants undamaged. Along with various seabirds, humpback whales and Hawai'ian monk seals can sometimes be spotted from the shore here. Near the point, the cobblestones underfoot once formed the surface of the old road. Ka'ena Point is a sacred site for the native Hawai'ians. Small shrines can be seen along the path, and, just past the point, is the sacred rock *Leina ka ʻuhane*, where souls are believed to break their earthly ties (see hike 26).

5. At the tip of Kaʻena Point, you are at the most westerly part of Oʻahu and can see the force of the Pacific Ocean as it divides around the island. Turn around and retrace your steps back to the parking lot at Kaʻena Point Park.

Wildlife

Look for humpback whales, which are famous for their haunting singing, from November to January, when they come to the area to mate and give birth. As well, the Laysan albatross (nicknamed "gooney bird") has returned to Kaʻena Point Natural Area Reserve and may be seen near the lighthouse at the point, where it has set up a nesting colony. Arriving in fall to begin its elaborate mating rituals, it stays for several months. Because this rare bird nests on the ground, with each pair's single egg taking two months to hatch, it is very vulnerable to predators. The wedge-tailed shearwater, reserve managers are pleased to announce, has also enjoyed a nesting resurgence here. Because this bird nests in burrows, staying on the trail helps avoid twisted ankles and injured nestlings.

Plants to Look For

beach naupaka (p. 176), 'ilima papa, pā'ū o Hi'iaka and pōhinahina (p. 176)

'Ilima papa

This extremely variable and widespread indigenous shrub remains low at the coast, though it can reach 10 feet in the mountains. Its deep yellow flowers, which are strongly associated with O'ahu, are popular for leis. The plant is also used medicinally.

Pā'ū o Hi'iaka

An indigenous woody morning glory of sunny leeward coastal areas, pā'ū o Hi'iaka has small, pale blue, violet or white flowers. Parts of the plant have had medicinal uses.

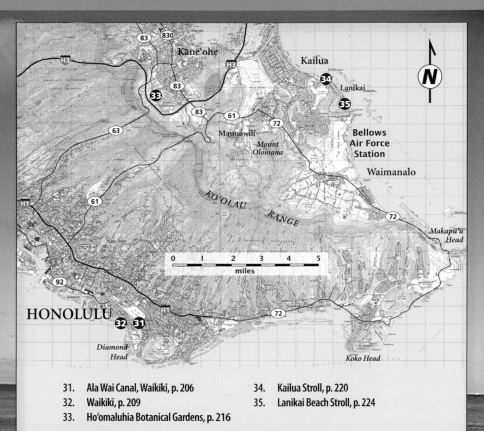

31. Ala Wai Canal, Waikīkī

Map: Waikīkī street map

Distance: 3.5 miles round trip

Time: 2 hours

Rating: easy

Elevation gain: none

Footwear: walking shoes

Best time and season: early morning, to avoid the midday heat; all seasons

Pictured here: Race day on the Canal

Highlights:

This walk provides an opportunity to enjoy the experience of this inner-city canal. On this peaceful and relatively uncrowded stroll, you may see outrigger teams practicing in the canal.

Trail Map

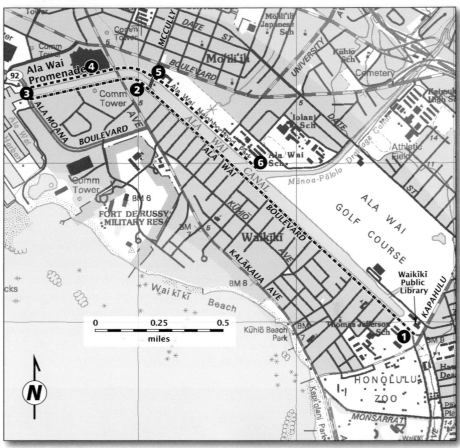

Stroll Description

Although we have made an arbitrary decision where to begin, you can start your walk anywhere on Ala Wai Boulevard.

1. Start at the corner of Kapahulu Avenue and Ala Wai Boulevard, adjacent to the Waikīkī Public Library, and head northwest on the paved walkway along the canal, away from Diamond Head.

2. Cross McCully Street and Kalākaua Avenue.

The Ala Wai Canal

Measuring 1.5 miles in length, the Ala Wai Canal was dredged in the 1920s to drain the surrounding area, which was then marshy, particularly during the rainy season. Without this project, Waikīkī would not be the tourist destination it is today. The canal is now the site of many outrigger races and canoe training sessions, and its banks are great for a pleasant stroll.

3. Make your way to Ala Moana Boulevard, where you cross the bridge to the other side of the canal. Be patient at the intersections—they are built for vehicles, not pedestrians, and there is a long wait for the pedestrian light. On the other side of the canal, you pick up a paved path, the Ala Wai Promenade.

4. Before you reach the next bridge, you pass the Hawaiʻi Convention Center on your left.

5. Cross McCully Street and pick up the path through Ala Wai Field.

6. Continue your stroll until you reach the Mānoa Pālolo Drainage Canal and the Ala Wai Golf Course. This is where public access on this side of the canal ends. The City of Honolulu has been considering closing the popular golf course, building on the land and extending the public path, but, as of this writing, progress has been slow. If you are lucky, you may find a canoeist willing to paddle you across the the canal; if not, retrace your steps to McCully Street and cross the McCully Street Bridge to complete your stroll.

Outrigger racing team

32. Waikīkī

Highlights:

During this urban stroll in Waikīkī ("spouting waters"), you can learn about Hawai'ian history as well as enjoy viewing several beautiful Waikīkī buildings.

Map: Waikīkī Street map

Distance: 2.5 miles

Time: 2 hours

Rating: easy

Elevation gain: none

Footwear: walking shoes

Best time and season: 5:45 PM to avoid the midday heat and crowds and to be in time for the changing of the guards at King's Village; all seasons

Trail Map

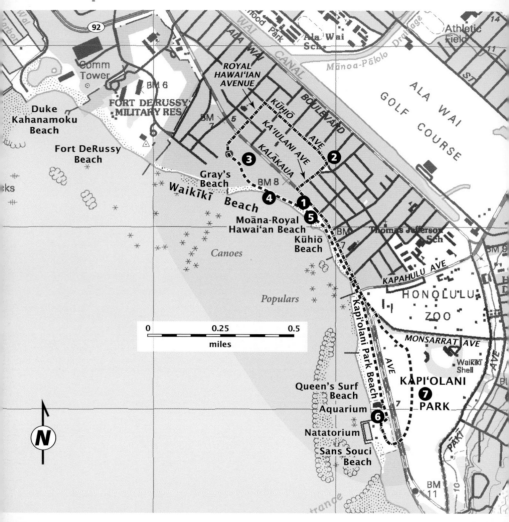

Duke Kahanamoku Beach

Fort DeRussy Beach

Comm Tower

BM 6

FORT DeRUSSY MILITARY RES.

BM 7

BM 5

ROYAL HAWAI'IAN AVENUE

KŪHIŌ AVE

KA'IULANI AVE

KALĀKAUA

ALA WAI CANAL

ALA WAI BOULEVARD

'ood Park

Ala Wai Sch.

Mānoa-Pālolo Drainage

ALA WAI GOLF COURSE

Athletic Field

92

Gray's Beach

Waikīkī Beach

BM 8

Moāna-Royal Hawai'an Beach

Kūhiō Beach

Thomas Jefferson Sch.

BM 7

Canoes

Populars

KAPAHULU AVE

HONOLULU ZOO

Kapi'olani Park Beach

MONSARRAT AVE

Waikīkī Shell

KAPI'OLANI PARK

Queen's Surf Beach

Aquarium

Natatorium

Sans Souci Beach

BM 11

0   0.25   0.5
miles

N

3 **2** **4** **1** **5** **6** **7**

Access

Begin your stroll at the Waikīkī Beach Center
located on Kalākaua Avenue, across the street from
the Hyatt Regency. From Waikīkī Beach Center,
walk *mauka* (away from the ocean) along Kaʻiulani
Avenue. On your right, at 131 Kaʻiulani Avenue, is
King's Village (formerly King's Alley).

1. King's Village

King's Village is located on the site of King David
Kalākaua's summer retreat; it houses a number of
quaint shops and features a beautiful mini courtyard surrounded by 19th-century-style buildings.
Here you can learn about Hawaiʻian royalty and
watch the colorful pageantry of the changing of the
guards. This free show occurs at the gate of King's
Village each evening at 6:15. After the show,
continue *mauka* (toward the mountains) and look
for the statue of Princess Kaʻiulani on the corner of
Kaʻiulani and Kūhiō Avenues.

Royal Hawaiʻian Hotel (above & center)

King's Village (below)

2. Statue of Princess Ka'iulani

Princess Victoria Ka'iulani's mother was Princess Miriam Likelike, sister to King Kalākaua, and her father was Archibald Cleghorn, the Scottish-born, one-time governor of O'ahu. At birth, Ka'iulani was given an estate called 'Ainahau in Waikīkī. It was near the ocean and surrounded by trees and flowers. Here, the young princess visited with author Robert Louis Stevenson, who had moved into the residence next door.

In 1891, shortly after ascending the throne, Queen Lili'uokalani named Princess Ka'iulani heir apparent to the Hawai'ian throne. But the monarchy was overthrown while the princess was visiting England. Upon her return, Hawai'i was a different place, now governed by the United States. Tragically, Princess Ka'iulani died in 1899, aged just 23, after being caught in a rainstorm while riding her horse on the Big Island. Turn left, walking away from Diamond Head, and continue on Kūhiō Avenue three blocks (counting on the left) until you reach Royal Hawai'ian Avenue. Turn *makai* (toward the ocean) and continue until you pass the Royal Hawai'ian Shopping Center. On the ocean side of the shopping center stands the Royal Hawai'ian Hotel, a beautiful building constructed of pink coral.

3. Royal Hawai'ian Hotel

Built as Waikīkī's first major hotel in 1927, the Royal Hawai'ian Hotel remains one of the most significant pieces of architecture on O'ahu. After visiting the gardens of the Royal Hawai'ian Hotel and wandering through the foyer (visitors are welcome inside the hotel), look for a path down to the ocean.

4. Waikīkī Beach

Once you are on the beach, stroll along it, going toward Diamond Head. Look for the famous surfing spot, Canoes, located out from the Royal Hawai'ian, and Populars, located out from Kūhiō Beach.

5. The Duke's Statue and Kūhiō Beach

Just toward Diamond Head from Waikīkī Beach Center, on the beachside path along Kalākaua Avenue, is the statue of Duke Kahanamoku. During the 1910s and '20s, the Duke was the world's fastest swimmer, winning three Olympic gold medals, two silvers and one bronze. Also fondly known as the "Father of Surfing," he was acclaimed a national hero for rescuing eight capsized fishermen off the California coast, thus beginning the tradition of lifeguards using surfboards. Duke Kahanamoku lived a full and long life, dying in 1968 at the age of 78.

Duke Kahanamoku—Hawai'i's greatest swimmer

Continue toward Diamond Head along Kalākaua Avenue. Look for the statue of Prince Jonah Kūhiō Kalanianaʻole (1871–1922) at Kūhiō Beach. Following Princess Kaʻiulani's death, Prince Kalanianaʻole would have inherited the throne after Queen Liliʻuokalani. However, the reigning monarch was overthrown in 1893. Prince Kalanianaʻole joined with his brother to try to restore the monarchy, but this attempt failed, and he was jailed for a year. Later, he worked to assist his people by spearheading the passage of the act that provided lands for native Hawaiʻians to homestead. March 26 is a territorial holiday in honor of Prince Kūhiō.

Continue toward Diamond Head to the sculpture *Makua and Kila*, also on the beach side of Kalākaua Avenue. Honoring ʻohana ("family") and the ocean, this sculpture of a boy and a Hawaiʻian monk seal was inspired by the story "Makua Lives on the Beach," which was written by noted surfer Fred Van Dyke.

At 5:00 PM on selected Saturdays and Sundays, the City and County of Honolulu and the Waikiki Improvement Association present "Sunset at the Beach" at Kūhiō

Prince Kūhiō (above), Makua and Kila (below)

Queen Kapiʻolani

Beach, at the foot of Kapahulu Avenue. This popular free event features live performances (cancelled in case of rain) followed at around 7:30 PM by a block-buster movie on a giant outdoor screen. Food and crafts are available for sale. For the schedule, ask at your hotel or check http://www.sunsetonthebeach.net/.

Your next stop is the statue *Surfer on a Wave*, with its 12 water jets, created in 2003 by local artist Robert Pashby. Continue until you reach Queen Kapiʻolani Park Beach Center, just before the Waikīkī Aquarium.

6. Queen's Beach

The beach in front of the aquarium is Queen's Beach. It was the site of the Queen's Retreat, named after the last ruling monarch of Hawaiʻi, Queen Liliʻuokalani. In the old days of the *kapu* system of laws, only the *aliʻi* ("aristocracy") were permitted on Waikīkī Beach; during her short reign, Queen Liliʻuokalani lifted the ban on commoners surfing and swimming here. The break in this bay is named "The Queen's" and is one of the most popular for surfers.

The impressive structure toward the beach is the War Memorial Natatorium. Completed in 1927, it commemorates the 102 Hawaiʻian servicemen killed in World War I. Four stone eagles top the 20-foot-tall archway. The facility was once a popular saltwater swimming pool and training site for Olympic contenders. After decades of neglect, the monument is slowly being restored. Cross Kalākaua Avenue to Queen Kapiʻolani Regional Park.

7. Queen Kapiʻolani Regional Park

Queen Kapiʻolani Regional Park has much to offer. It is a popular running and walking area. Also, each Saturday and Sunday, from 9:00 AM to 4:00 PM, the park features "Art at the Zoo Fence," where you can meet artists and buy their works. As well, there is a torch lighting ceremony, with Hawaiʻian music and hula, at the Kapiʻolani Beach Park Center each Saturday and Sunday at 6:45 PM. The popular Kodak Hula Show at the Waikīkī Shell, begun in 1937, has ended because of a lack of funds.

For more information, check the park directory at the corner of Kalākaua and Kapahulu Avenues, adjacent to the

Honolulu Zoo entrance. Near the park directory, look for the burial-ground monument, *Ka Halia Aloha*, the place of loving remembrance for Hawai'ians. Before leaving the park, visit the nearby statue of India's pacifist "Father of the Nation," Mahatma Gandhi.

More to See

'Iolani Palace and the State Capitol Building

For another historical walk, take a bus or walk 4 miles *ewa* (west) from Waikīkī to 'Iolani Palace, located along South King Street between Punchbowl and Richards Streets. In this area, you can also visit the King Kamehameha I statue (across South King from the palace), the State Capitol Building (just north of the palace) and the historic Kawaiaha'o Church (957 Punchbowl Street) and stroll through Chinatown (about 5 blocks *ewa* along South King from the palace) and the Foster Botanical Garden (about 5 blocks

mauka (toward the mountains) from Chinatown; enter from Vineyard Boulevard, just west of Nu'uanu Street). Honolulu is a city with history and beauty, not just a sunbathers' paradise.

Know the Names of the Beaches
From east to west, the beaches are Queen's Surf, Kūhiō, Moāna-Royal Hawai'an, Gray's, Fort DeRussy and Duke Kahanamoku.

War Memorial Natatorium (above)

33. Ho'omaluhia Botanical Gardens

Map: USGS Kāne'ohe

Distance: 1 to 2 miles

Time: 1 to 3 hours, depending on time spent viewing the gardens

Rating: easy

Elevation gain: none

Footwear and special equipment: walking shoes

Best time and season: all seasons

Distance from Waikīkī to trailhead: approx. 12 miles

Hours of operation: open daily 9:00 AM to 4:00 PM, except Christmas and New Year's

Highlights

This 400-acre botanical garden includes many rare and endangered plants, both Hawai'ian and from around the world—Africa, Philippines, Sri Lanka, India, Polynesia, Melanesia, Malaysia and Tropical America. It is beautifully laid out and ideal for a relaxed stroll.

Access Map

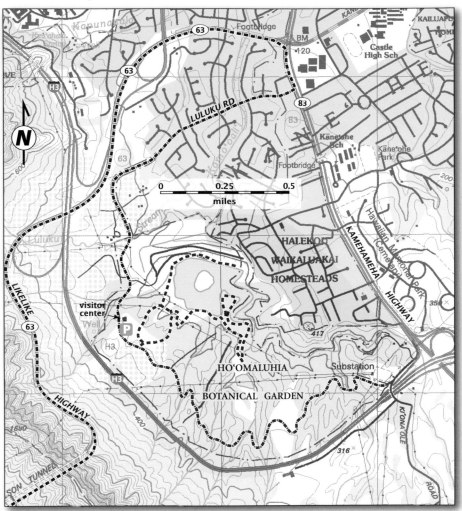

Access from Waikīkī to Trailhead

Take McCully Street *mauka* (toward the mountains) across the Lunalilo Freeway (H-1) and go left onto the H-1 westbound. Pass the Pali Highway (SR 61) and take exit 20A for the Likelike Highway (SR 63), exiting to your right. Drive across the Koʻolua Range to the windward side of Oʻahu.

Pass the intersection with the John A. Burns Freeway (H-3) and then turn right onto the Kamehameha Highway (SR 83) at Puohala Village.

Almost immediately, after you pass Windward City Shopping Center on the left, turn right on Luluku Road. Continue on Luluku Road through the entrance of Hoʻomaluhia Gardens until you reach the

Trail Map

visitor center and parking area. For information, call (808) 233-7323 or visit the website at http://www.honolulu.gov/parks/hbg/hmbg.htm.

Trail Description

This botanical garden is one of five gardens that make up the Honolulu Botanical Gardens, which are supported by the Department of Parks and Recreation of the City and the County of Honolulu. Ho'omaluhia was originally built by the U.S. Army Corps of Engineers to provide flood protection for Kāne'ohe. *Ho'omaluhia* means "to make a place of peace and tranquility." The garden offers a number of facilities and programs, including the visitors' center, picnic and camping areas, and nature programs.

Pick up a map at the visitors' center, begin your stroll on the paved road and then branch off on any of the many walking trails through the garden. Follow the posted warnings about handling unfamiliar plants, because some are poisonous.

Guided nature walks take place at 10:00 AM each Saturday and 1:00 PM on Sundays. Call (808) 233-7323 to register.

Non-native Plants

Unbelievably, introduced plants now outnumber Hawai'i's rich variety of native plants. Invasive plants brought in by humans change the environment, cause economic loss and compete with native flora and fauna. Currently in Hawai'i, alien pests including plants, animals, insects and diseases are arriving at an unprecedented rate. Before humans populated the islands, one new species arrived once every 35,000 years. Now 20 to 30 new species turn up annually.

You can help stop non-native species from entering and spreading in Hawai'i. Remember to clean your hiking boots, dogs, camping gear and car tires before entering a native forest or traveling between islands, because mud often carries alien weeds. Also, turn unwanted pets in to the Humane Society because pets and aquarium plants released into the wild compete with or prey on native plants and animals. For more ideas, visit the *State of Hawaii's Invasive Species Watch* website at: http://www.state.hi.us/dlnr/isw/iswhome.htm.

34. Kailua Stroll

Map: USGS Kāneʻohe and a Kailua Street map (for example, from *Rand McNally Street Guide: Oʻahu*)

Distance: 1 mile

Time: 1 hour

Rating: easy beach stroll

Elevation gain: none

Footwear and special equipment: walking shoes

Best time and season: arrive at the park early in the morning, especially on weekends or holidays, in order to secure a parking space at Kailua Beach Park

Distance from Waikīkī to trailhead: approx. 15.5 miles

Highlights

The little Hawaiʻian town of Kailua is famous for its windsurfers and for its peace and quiet.

Access from Waikīkī to Trailhead

Take McCully Street *mauka* (toward the mountains) across the Lunalilo Freeway (H-1) and go left onto the

Access Map

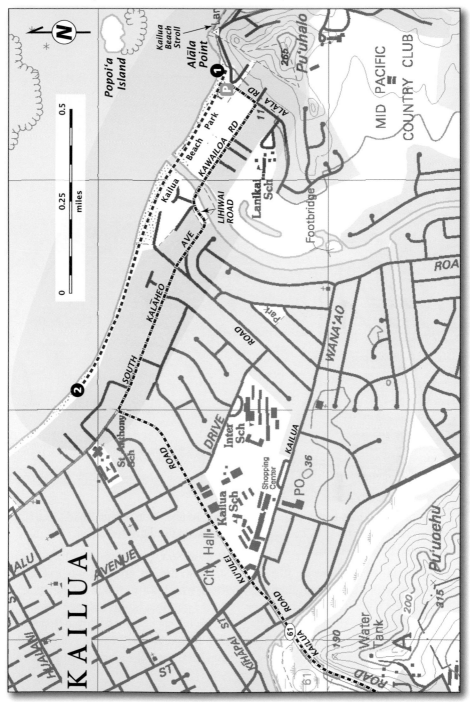

Trail Map

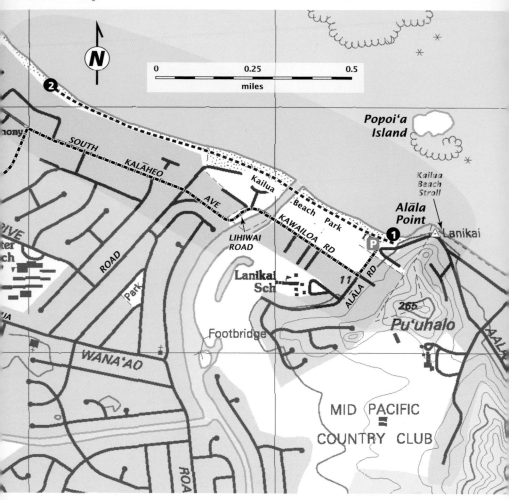

H-1 westbound. From the H-1, turn right on the Pali Highway (SR 61) at exit 21B and pass the Pali Lookout.

Continue on the Pali Highway; after the intersection with Auloa Road and the Kamehameha Highway (SR 83), you are on the Kalaniana'ole Highway (SR 61). Where the Kalaniana'ole Highway (SR 72) turns right opposite the Castle Medical Center (on your left), proceed straight ahead on Kailua Road (SR 61), following the signs to Kailua.

At a four-way intersection with Oneawa Street on the left, go straight onto Ku'ulei Road, which soon ends at a T-junction. Turn right onto South Kalāheo Avenue, which briefly becomes Lihiwai Road and then Kawailoa Road before you cross the canal and park at Kailua Beach Park.

Trail Description

1. From the beach park, go northwest (to your left) along the beach. You are likely to see experienced windsurfers crossing Kailua Bay, especially on windy days. The point to your left is Makapu Pennisula, where the Kāne'ohe Marine Corps is located.

2. When you reach the end of the public beach, retrace your steps back to Kailua Beach Park.

Kailu Beach with Makapu Pennisula in the background (above), beach flowers (below)

35. Lanikai Beach Stroll

Map: USGS Kāne'ohe and a Lanikai Street map (for example, from *Rand McNally Street Guide: O'ahu*)

Distance: 1 mile

Time: 1 hour

Rating: easy beach stroll

Elevation gain: none

Footwear and special equipment: walking shoes

Best time and season: weekday mornings are best for finding parking in Lanikai; any season

Distance from Waikīkī to trailhead: approx. 17 miles

Highlights

Lanikai has been rated as one of the most beautiful beaches in the world. It is a credit to the State of Hawai'i that the amazing sand beaches of O'ahu remain open to the public, unlike so many famous beaches around the world. Among the attractions are watching

Access Map

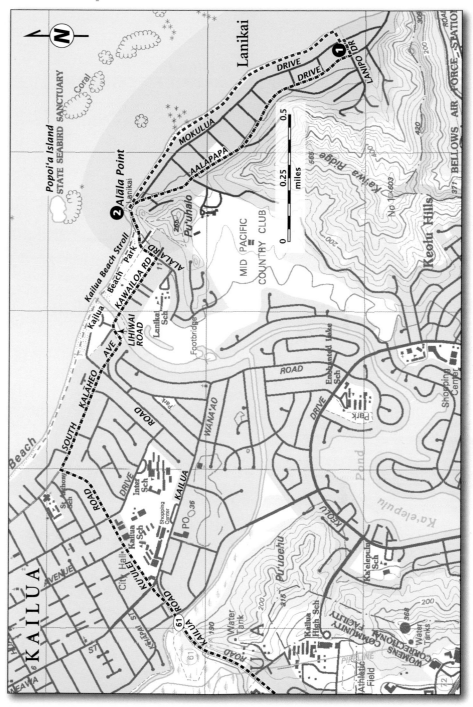

Trail Map

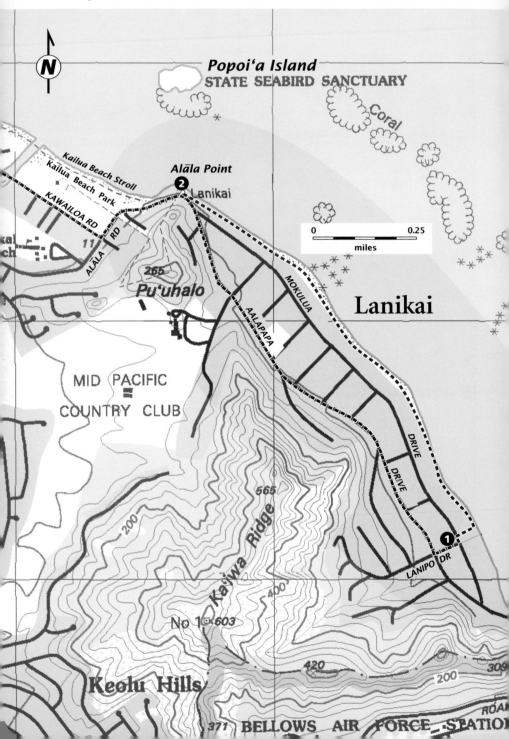

Popoi'a Island
STATE SEABIRD SANCTUARY

Coral

Kailua Beach Stroll

Kailua Beach Park

KAWAILOA RD

Alāla Point

❷ Lanikai

ALALA RD

11

265

Pu'uhalo

MOKULUA

Lanikai

AALAPAPA

0　　　　0.25
miles

MID PACIFIC
COUNTRY CLUB

565

DRIVE

DRIVE

❶

LANIPO DR

Ka'iwa Ridge

200

400

No 1 603

420

200

309

Keolu Hills

371

BELLOWS AIR FORCE STATION

ROAD

the windsurfers, trying to spot the green turtles that swim along this beach and enjoying the cool winds on this side of the island.

Access from Waikīkī to Trailhead

Take McCully Street *mauka* (toward the mountains) across the Lunalilo Freeway (H-1) and go left onto the H-1 westbound. From the H-1, turn right on the Pali Highway (SR 61) at exit 21B and pass the Pali Lookout.

Continue on the Pali Highway; after the intersection with Auloa Road and the Kamehameha Highway (SR 83), you are on the Kalaniana'ole Highway (SR 61).

Where the Kalaniana'ole Highway (SR 72) turns right opposite the Castle Medical Center (on your left), proceed straight ahead on Kailua Road (SR 61), following the signs to Kailua.

At a four-way intersection with Oneawa Street on the left, go straight onto Ku'ulei Road, which soon ends at a T junction. Turn right onto South Kalāheo Avenue, which briefly becomes Lihiwai Road and then Kawailoa Road before you cross the canal at Kailua Beach Park and turn left onto Alāla Road.

Where the road forks into one-way streets, you bear right onto Aalapapa Drive and continue through the little

Green Sea Turtle

This reptile, known as *honu* in Hawai'ian, lives in the ocean feeding on bottom-dwelling grasses and algae. Female turtles come ashore once a year to lay eggs (usually on a secluded beach). The eggs develop over two months, and the little hatchlings dig themselves out and make a mad dash to the water. Only two to five percent survive the predators and other threats. An adult can live to 80 years, weigh over 400 pounds and measure up to 5 feet in length! Please give these turtles the respect they deserve, and keep at least 10 feet back if you encounter any.

community of Lanikai until you reach Lanipo Drive. Park in this general area. Lanikai is usually a safe place to park, but you may have trouble finding a parking space on the street.

Trail Description

1. Walk toward the ocean on Lanipo Street and go left onto Mokulua Drive. There are several public access points along Mokulua. Take the first access to the ocean and begin your stroll to your left (northwest) along this beautiful beach. In the bay are two nature reserves, the Mokulua Islands of Moku Nu (most northerly; restricted access) and Moku Iki (no access). As you walk, you may be among the few fortunate beach walkers to spot a green sea turtle in the ocean. Several outrigger teams train from this beach, including the women's team— *Na Wahine Ho Ho Honi*, meaning "Swift Strong Women." Look for their boats along the beach or, if you are fortunate, you may see them training in the bay.

2. Stroll until the public beach ends near Alāla Point. The island offshore here, Popoi'a ("rotted fish") Island, also known as Flat Island, is another seabird sanctuary. Turn and retrace your walk.

References

Allen, Helena G. 1982. *The Betrayal of Liliuokalani—Last Queen of Hawaii, 1838–1917*. Mutual Publishing, Honolulu.

Ball, Stuart M., Jr. 2000. *The Hikers Guide to Oʻahu* (revised edition). University of Hawaiʻi Press, Honolulu.

Beckwith, Martha W. 1989. *Hawaiian Mythology*. University of Hawaiʻi Press, Honolulu.

Beletsky, Les. 2000. *Hawaii: The Ecotravellers' Wildlife Guide*. Academic Press, San Diego.

Department of Lands & Natural Resources. 2001. *Na Ala Hele—Hiking Safely in Hawaiʻi*. Division of Forestry & Wildlife, Hawaiʻi.

Hawaii Audubon Society. 1993. *Hawaii's Birds*. Hawaii Audubon Society, Honolulu.

Miyano, Leland. 1997. *Hawaiʻi's Beautiful Trees*. Mutual Publishing, Honolulu.

Miyano, Leland. 2002. *A Pocket Guide to Hawaiʻi's Flowers*. Mutual Publishing, Honolulu.

Pratt, H. Douglas. 2000. *A Pocket Guide to Hawaiʻi's Trees and Shrubs*. Mutual Publishing, Honolulu.

Trail #	Trail	Distance	Time in hours	Rating	Elevation Gain
	HONOLULU				
1	Diamond Head	1.6 miles out and back	1.5	moderate	560 ft.
2	Makiki Valley Loop	2.5 mile loop	3	moderate	800 ft.
3	Moleka and ʻUalakaʻa Trails	1.3 miles round trip	1	easy	350 ft.
4	Mānoa Cliff Loop	6 mile loop	5	moderate	880 ft.
5	Mānoa Falls	1.6 miles out and back	1.5	easy	600 ft.
6	ʻAihualama to Nuʻuanu Overlook	3.2 miles out and back	2	moderate	1200 ft.
7	Judd Memorial Trail and Jackass Ginger Pool	1 mile loop	2	easy	250 ft.
8	ʻAihualama to Judd Memorial Trail	4.3 miles one way	2.5	moderate	1200 ft.
9	Puʻu Ohia & Pauoa Flats to Nuʻuanu Lookout	3 miles	3	moderate	100 ft.
10	Waʻahila Ridge	2.8 miles out and back	2.5	moderate	900 ft.
11	Lanipo Mauʻumae	5 miles out and back	3	challenging	1100 ft.
12	Wiliwilinui	3 miles out and back	2.5	moderate	400 ft.
13	Kuliʻouʻou Ridge	5 miles out and back	4	moderate to steep	1800 ft.
14	Kuliʻouʻou Valley	1.2 miles out and back	45 minutes	easy	300 ft.
15	Koko Crater Botanical Gardens	0.3 mile loop	1	easy	relatively flat

Best Time and Season	Distance Waikīkī to Trailhead	Notes and Cautions	Page #
early morning; all seasons	4 mi.	Fees. Hours: 6 AM to 6 PM. Note: includes steep uphill section	20
all seasons	3.5 mi.	Hours: Hawai'i Nature Center road closes at 6 PM. Caution: trail slippery when raining	27
all seasons	7 mi.		33
all seasons	7 mi.		38
early morning (to avoid peak times); after rainfall (falls more spectacular)	3 mi.	Caution: heavy downpours cause rockfalls; trail may be closed with heavy rain	44
morning (to avoid crowds); all seasons	3 mi.	One steep, rocky section. Caution: trail slippery in heavy rain	48
any time or season	8 mi.	Includes two stream crossings on boulders. Caution: trail to the pool slippery in rainy weather	52
morning (to avoid crowds); all seasons	3 mi.	Arrange for transportation at Judd Memorial Trailhead. Note: trail includes one steep, rocky section and one stream crossing on boulders. Caution: slippery in rain	58
all seasons	7 mi.		64
all seasons	4 mi.	Includes one steep boulder climb. Caution: trail slippery in the rain	69
all seasons	6 mi.	Includes narrow, steep ridge walk Caution: trail slippery when wet	74
all seasons	8 mi.	Free parking permit required. Caution: route along the ridge is slippery during rainfall	80
all seasons	8 mi.	Caution: narrow ridge on the last stretch	84
all seasons	8 mi.	Could combine with hike 13	90
spring	13.5 mi.	No charge. Hours: 9 AM to 4 PM daily; closed Christmas and New Year's	94

Trail #	Trail	Distance	Time in hours	Rating	Elevation Gain
	EAST OAHU				
16	Makapuʻu State Wayside	2 miles out and back	1.5	easy	520 ft.
17	Maunawili Falls	2.5 miles out and back	2.5	moderate	400 ft.
18	Maunawili Demonstration Trail	8 miles one way (10.5 miles— Pali Lookout to Waimanalo bus stop)	5	moderate	650-ft. descent
19	Old Pali Road	2 miles out and back	1	easy	350 ft.
20	Kapaʻeleʻele Loop	1 mile loop	30 minutes	easy	100 ft.
21	Hauʻula	2.5 mile loop	2	easy	700 ft.
22	Maʻakua Ridge Loop	2.5 miles out and back, plus loop	2.5	easy	800 ft.
23	Lāʻie Falls	7 miles out and back	4	moderate to difficult	600 ft.
	NORTH SHORE				
24	Kaunala and Puʻu o Mahuka Heiau	3 mile loop	3	moderate	600 ft.
25	Keālia and Kuaokalā Ridge	12 miles out and back, including Kuaokalā Ridge loop	5	moderate to difficult	2000 ft.
26	Kaʻena Point North	5 miles out and back	3.5	easy	none

Best Time and Season	Distance Waikīkī to Trailhead	Notes and Cautions	Page #
October to May for possible whale sightings	13 mi.		100
all seasons; avoid during heavy rainstorms	11 mi.	Pets not allowed on this trail. Caution: several stream crossings that can be hazardous, especially during or following heavy rainfall	107
waterfalls look best after rainfall	10 mi.	Arrange for transportation at Waimanalo trailhead at end of hike. Caution: heavy rains may cause flooding	113
all seasons	9 mi.		122
all seasons	30 mi.		127
all seasons	33 mi.	As of this writing, Maʻakua Gulch Trail is closed (flash flood dangers). Caution: includes two stream crossings on rocks that can be slippery during or after heavy rain	132
all seasons	33 mi.	As of this writing, Maʻakua Gulch Trail is closed (flash flood dangers)	138
closed on Sundays; all seasons	36 mi.	Permits required. Caution: first section is eroded and difficult in rainy weather; also, use extreme caution or avoid the steep hike down to the falls during or after heavy rainfalls—flash flood danger	145
all seasons	46.5 mi.	Hours: open only on weekends and holidays, from daybreak to sunset	152
morning; winter (cooler)	44 mi.	Hours: gate to Dillingham Airport is open from 7 AM to 6 PM daily. Caution: trail includes ridge walk with steep slopes	160
winter or spring (cooler); fall and winter best for wildlife (see hike 30)	51 mi.	To protect the wildlife at the point, do not bring any pets on this hike. Prepare for heat: entire route is in the sun. Caution: waves can be fierce; never turn your back on the sea when close to the water—you could be swept out to sea	170

Trail #	Trail	Distance	Time in hours	Rating	Elevation Gain
	WEST-CENTRAL OAHU				
27	'Aiea Loop: Keaīwa Heiau State Park	4.3 mile loop	2.5	moderate	900 ft.
28	Waimano	2 miles round trip	1	easy	300 ft.
29	Kuaokalā Ridge Loop	5.5 mile loop	3.5 to 4	moderate to difficult	600 ft.
30	Ka'ena Point South	5 miles out and back	3.5	easy	none
	URBAN STROLLS				
31	Ala Wai Canal, Waikīkī	3.5 miles round trip	2	easy	none
32	Waikīkī	2.5 miles	2	easy	none
33	Ho'omaluhia Botanical Gardens	1 to 2 miles	1 to 3	easy	none
34	Kailua Stroll	1 mile	1	easy beach stroll	none
35	Lanikai Beach Stroll	1 mile	1	easy beach stroll	none

Best Time and Season	Distance Waikīkī to Trailhead	Notes and Cautions	Page #
all seasons	16 mi.	Hours: 7 AM to 7:45 PM (April 1 to Labor Day); closes at 6:45 PM the rest of the year	178
all seasons	16 mi.		185
winter (cooler)	44 mi.	Permit required. Caution: trail includes ridge walk with steep slopes; also, do not hike off the trail into the Mākua Valley (used as a military range)	191
winter or spring (cooler); fall and winter best for wildlife	45 mi.	To protect the wildlife at the point, do not bring any pets on this hike. Prepare for heat: entire route is in the sun. Caution: waves can be fierce; never turn your back on the sea when close to the water—you could be swept out to sea	198
early morning; all seasons			206
5:45 PM (avoid heat and crowds and catch changing of guards at King's Village); all seasons			209
all seasons	12 mi.	Hours: open daily 9 AM to 4 PM, except Christmas and New Year's	216
early in morning, especially on weekends or holidays (for parking at Kailua Beach Park)	15.5 mi.		220
weekday mornings (best for parking in Lanikai); any season	17 mi.		224

Trail Name	Trail #	Page #	Region
'Aiea Loop: Keaīwa Heiau State Park	27	178	West-Central O'ahu
'Aihualama to Judd Memorial Trail	8	58	Honolulu
'Aihualama to Nu'uanu Overlook	6	48	Honolulu
Ala Wai Canal, Waikīkī	31	206	Urban Strolls
Diamond Head	1	20	Honolulu
Hau'ula	21	132	East O'ahu
Ho'omaluhia Botanical Gardens	33	216	Urban Strolls
Judd Memorial Trail and Jackass Ginger Pool	7	52	Honolulu
Ka'ena Point North	26	170	North Shore
Ka'ena Point South	30	198	West-Central O'ahu
Kailua Stroll	34	220	Urban Strolls
Kapa'ele'ele Loop	20	127	East O'ahu
Kaunala and Pu'u o Mahuka Heiau	24	152	North Shore
Keālia and Kuaokalā Ridge	25	160	North Shore
Koko Crater Botanical Gardens	15	94	Honolulu
Kuaokala Ridge Loop	29	191	West-Central O'ahu
Kuli'ou'ou Ridge	13	84	Honolulu
Kuli'ou'ou Valley	14	90	Honolulu
Lā'ie Falls	23	145	East O'ahu
Lanikai Beach Stroll	35	224	Urban Strolls
Lanipo Mau'umae	11	74	Honolulu
Ma'akua Ridge Loop	22	138	East O'ahu
Makapu'u State Wayside	16	100	East O'ahu
Makiki Valley Loop	2	27	Honolulu
Mānoa Cliff Loop	4	38	Honolulu
Mānoa Falls	5	44	Honolulu
Maunawili Demonstration Trail	18	113	East O'ahu
Maunawili Falls	17	107	East O'ahu
Moleka and 'Ualaka'a Trails	3	33	Honolulu
Old Pali Road	19	122	East O'ahu
Pu'u Ohia and Pauoa Flats to Nu'uanu Lookout	9	64	Honolulu
Wa'ahila Ridge	10	69	Honolulu
Waikīkī	32	209	Urban Strolls
Waimano	28	185	West-Central O'ahu
Wiliwilinui	12	80	Honolulu

Index of Plants

Boldface type indicates featured species with detailed descriptions.

NI'IHAU **KAUA'I**

Kapa'a
Hanamaulu
Kekaha • Lihue
Kalaheo

O'AHU

Lā'ie
Waialua • Hau'ula
• Hale'iwa •
Wahiawā
Mākaha • Kahalu'u
Waipahu • • Mokapu
• Pearl • Kailua
'Aiea
Ewa • • Waimanalo
Ewa ★
Beach **Honolulu**

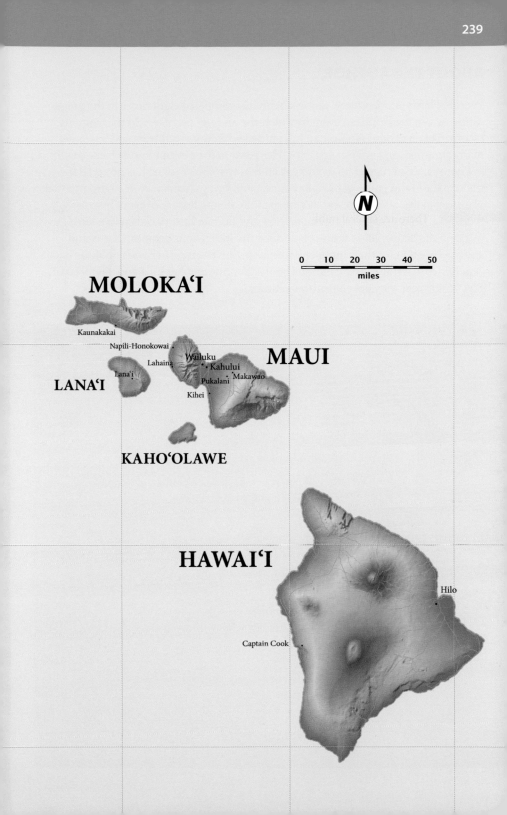

N

```
0    10   20   30   40   50
|----|----|----|----|----|
         miles
```

MOLOKAʻI

Kaunakakai

Napili-Honokowai

Wailuku

Lahaina

MAUI

Lana'i

Kahului

Pukalani

Makawao

LANAʻI

Kihei

KAHOʻOLAWE

HAWAIʻI

Hilo

Captain Cook

ABOUT THE AUTHOR

Yvonne Harris is a marathon canoeist who has competed eight times in the longest canoe race in the world, an event in which she and her partner held the women's record. This avid outdoorswoman has guided whitewater raft trips and has spent many summers on family canoe trips. Her passion for extreme sports blends with her enjoyment of rugged hikes and casual family walks. Yvonne has hiked all the trails in the Oʻahu guide, some many times, and brings her career in environmental planning to the carefully researched maps that are the feature of every hike in this book. Deeply interested in the natural and human history of Hawaiʻi, her work on the hiking guide shows respect for the indigenous people of the island and appreciation for the natural environment. She has used her wide outdoor experience to write several children's books. Yvonne and her husband, Paul Harris, now reside near Vancouver, British Columbia.